IT TAKES One TO TANGO

How I Rescued My Marriage
with (Almost) No Help from My Spouse—
and How You Can, Too

WINIFRED M. REILLY, MA, MFT

TOUCHSTONE
New York London Toronto Sydney New Delhi

Touchstone
An Imprint of Simon & Schuster, Inc.
1230 Avenue of the Americas
New York, NY 10020

First Touchstone hardcover edition April 2017

TOUCHSTONE and colophon are registered trademarks
of Simon & Schuster, Inc.

For information about special discounts for bulk purchases,
please contact Simon & Schuster Special Sales at 1-866-506-1949
or business@simonandschuster.com.

The Simon & Schuster Speakers Bureau can bring authors to
your live event. For more information or to book an event, contact
the Simon & Schuster Speakers Bureau at 1-866-248-3049
or visit our website at www.simonspeakers.com.

Interior design by Jill Putorti

Manufactured in the United States of America

10 9 8 7 6 5 4 3 2 1

Library of Congress Cataloging-in-Publication Data is available.

ISBN 978-1-5011-2582-9
ISBN 978-1-5011-2587-4 (ebook)

To my extraordinary teachers
Ellyn Bader
and James W. Maddock,
who inspired me to take bold steps in my life and in my work

and to my husband, Patrick,
who bore the brunt of this boldness with love and, eventually, grace.

New love is the brightest, and long love is the greatest;
but revived love is the tenderest thing known upon earth.

—THOMAS HARDY

CONTENTS

CONTENTS

AUTHOR'S NOTE

The examples and case studies I refer to throughout the book are drawn from my practice. I have changed all the names and identifying details. Some stories are composites. I have, however, made sure to accurately represent the dynamics of these relationships. My own story is true.

IT TAKES
One
TO TANGO

INTRODUCTION

There's a Turkish proverb that says, "No matter how far you have gone on a wrong road, turn back." I find this notion deeply comforting: that things can change, that people can turn their lives around, that it's never too late to try. Even if the clock is about to strike midnight. Even if their car's in a ditch and they're almost out of gas.

When I sit with a couple in trouble, I'm often the only one in the room who has any hope at all for their marriage. Hope is what gives people a reason to keep going. Hope fuels the faith that there's still someplace worth going to. And unfortunately, hope is one of the first things to go when a marriage hits rough terrain.

I'm amazed at how long people will suffer in dreadful relationships believing that there's no help to be found. Five, eight, ten years. Sometimes even longer. Some have been deemed "incurable" by a previous therapist who simply didn't have the skills to effectively guide them. Some believe their spouse is to blame for their difficulties; often that spouse appears to be unwilling to change. Some think they're too damaged, that they're not marriage material, or that marriage is, in and of itself impossible to do well. Many fear that the mess they've made of their marriage is too big to clean up.

Fortunately, I know something that they don't.

I know that even the most troubled marriages can be repaired—not just patched up but truly transformed. Not in ten simple steps. Not without focus and determination. And not without challenging much of the conventional wisdom about what it really takes to turn a marriage around.

Most people believe that marriage should be easier than it is. It's one of the great myths—that marriage is supposed to be blissful, that only troubled people have trouble, that healthy, well-meaning people who love each other won't have to work all that hard. When couples hit the hard challenges that *all* couples hit, many get discouraged. Most assume that something has gone terribly wrong.

Back in the early, struggle-filled years of my own marriage, I needed a new way of thinking about our difficulties as much as I needed practical skills. Like many couples who are bogged down by conflict, I thought my husband and I were worse off than most—the two of us ready to fight to the death about anything and everything, both of us fiercely convinced we were right and unable (or unwilling) to admit when we weren't. I was critical. He brooded. I was inclined to slam doors. His look of disdain left me feeling three inches tall. Our fights were followed by days of hurt feelings and estrangement that our pathetic attempts at repair were unable to heal.

How did we get here? I often wondered, longing for the days when we'd been loving and close. Marriage couldn't possibly be as difficult for others as it was for us. Surely others knew something about being happily married that we'd not yet figured out.

This I believed despite dismal divorce rates, quarreling neighbors, and a steady stream of unhappy couples seeking my help, and despite the fact that our friends' marriages were dissolving one after the other. I knew I wanted to stay married—no, not just married but joyfully, wholeheartedly-glad-that-I-married-you married—but I wasn't sure how. And in the darkest of times, I feared that our chances were slim, at best.

My husband and I slogged on for years, bickering, sulking, making peace—until next time. Nothing I learned in my years of clinical training, in the many workshops I attended and the countless books that I read, or in the dozens of hours we spent in couples therapy explained why we were stuck—or, more crucial still, what would unstick us. No one told me the one thing that would have helped me the most: "It isn't just you. Marriage is hard."

Marriage puts two people into a small space, with the intention of keeping them there for a lifetime, and then says, "Good luck!" Marriage doesn't come with a guidebook or a road map to make our journey easier. And none of us steps into marriage with all the tools we need for success. We simply hit the ground running, and despite our good intentions and optimism, for most of us marriage ends up being far more difficult to navigate than we'd expected. But that doesn't mean something is wrong; it simply means that marriage is a tough teacher and we all have plenty to learn.

INTRODUCTION

Most couples are surprised (and relieved) when I tell them that struggle in marriage is not only normal, it's *necessary*. The struggles we face are the very things that help us develop the strength and capacity to be successfully married, especially if we're willing to learn the lessons they offer us. The way we fight and the things we fight about (or the way that, in some cases, we avoid conflict at all costs) reveal both our strengths and our weaknesses. They show how poorly or well we advocate for ourselves, whether we're rigid or flexible, whether we get our way by sulking or bullying, whether we too quickly collapse. They point to our dreams and desires and to the frustrations we face in attaining them. And they dare us to reach and to risk, even in the face of our partner's opposition.

Marriages move through predictable stages of development, beginning with the sweet harmony of courtship and moving through the unsettling and often turbulent encounters with differences that follow. Couples either rise to the challenges they face at each stage or find themselves frustrated and stuck, fighting the same fights, hitting the same logjams—never reaching the later stages of deeper intimacy and connection they hoped marriage would bring.

Sadly, there's where a lot of couples give up.

Sure, some marriages aren't sustainable. When there's physical violence or serious drug or alcohol use, when there are repeated betrayals of trust, or when someone gambles or lies compulsively and refuses to get help, it makes good sense to leave. And some people decide that, sustainable or not, the problems in their marriage aren't ones they care to surmount.

But a vast majority of struggling couples *want* to stay married. Too often, though, they divorce because they simply can't find a way to live happily with their spouse. Worse, they settle for a far-from-ideal marriage, concluding that a mediocre marriage is better than none. Some grow bitter and angry, feeling stymied by a partner who is unwilling to change or to grow. Others try everything they can think of to create change, growing more and more discouraged each time they fail. Most lack the tools to move forward effectively. Most believe that forward movement is out of their hands.

Few of them realize that they have more power than they think.

The party line about marriage—what I was repeatedly told by marriage therapists and books—is that it takes two, that marriage is a two-way street, a fifty-fifty proposition, that successful couples are those who are willing to meet each other halfway. We're told that marital change is contingent upon couples having a shared commitment to growth and that for good things to happen *both* partners must be willing to put both feet into the process.

If it takes two people to fix things, what happens when one partner is deeply discouraged or has one foot out the door? Or when one partner is desperately longing for change and the other digs in his heels? Does that mean the more optimistic partner should just call it quits?

Like the countless other mismatches we face as couples (sex twice a week / sex once in a blue moon, squirrel away every penny / live while you can), frequently one partner is more committed, more hopeful, more open to change, or more determined to save the marriage than the other. Sometimes there's no way to sell "improvement" to a spouse who thinks things are good enough as they are, believes she's an innocent bystander in the marriage's troubles, or behaves outrageously and feels entitled to be loved "as is."

Rather than live miserably, give up, or drive yourself nuts, consider this alternative: if your spouse won't join you in changing your marriage, do it yourself.

I know what you're thinking: it only works when two people are willing to try. You're already doing more than your fair share, and now you're being asked to do even *more*! You've compromised, begged, and bitten your tongue. You've been assertive and accommodating and gone well past halfway. Besides, you're not the person who's been such a jerk.

I hear it all the time from readers and clients and even some colleagues who still subscribe to the "two to tango" philosophy: Why should *one* person do all the hard work while the other just sits on her duff?

The problem with this way of thinking is that it leaves you with options that only make matters worse. Say your partner refuses to carry his or her weight—will things *really* be better if you match that sorry effort just to make it more fair? You might try lowering your standards and resigning yourself to live life as it miserably is. Or you can try, yet again, to get that difficult, hunkered-down spouse of yours to be enthused about change. Chances are, you'll end up back at square one: worn out, discouraged, and one step closer to thinking the only way out of your difficult marriage is divorce.

In this book I'll show you a new way of thinking—one that will help you make sense of why you're stuck and enable you to get moving. I'll explain how one steady and determined partner, acting alone, can create far-reaching positive change, often accomplishing change in a marriage that cannot be made any other way. I'll help you see why it's essential to let go of your concerns about fairness and the need for both partners to work as a team, and I'll empower you to sign on to being the front-runner for change. Without feeling burdened. Without settling. And without needing your spouse to read this book, too.

I'll teach you how to unhook from the maddening, repetitive struggles that have left you feeling wiped out, worn down, or boiling with rage. I'll show you how to take a firm stand for what truly matters to you, without arguing, cajoling, or resorting to threats; and how to set clear goals for yourself—and successfully work to achieve them. You'll learn to stop getting thrown off and worked up about your spouse's unproductive (and even destructive) behaviors and to calmly focus on the one thing you have the power to change: yourself.

I know from experience that when one partner takes that first step, goes out on a limb, behaves in a new way, challenges the status quo, the other will usually follow. Sometimes slowly, not always cheerfully, and often not in the way we imagined. But eventually both partners become stronger and healthier, and so does the marriage.

Though this book is founded on well-proven psychological theory—something I'll discuss later in the book—it's not a theoretical text. Nor is it a typical self-help book. This book comes from my personal experience, from my own trial-and-error process of trying to keep my troubled marriage from coming apart. It tells my story and the story of many couples I've worked with. It weaves in brain science, family systems theory, and the psychology of couple development, making it clear why if you want to be close and connected to your spouse, it's crucial for you to be able to act alone. Even better, it suggests how you can launch—and sustain—your own marriage remodel, whether or not your spouse joins in the effort.

No matter how far down a wrong path your marriage has gone, it's not too late to turn back. You can strike out in a different direction; you can blaze a new trail. It's my hope that you'll use this book as a map to help you and your spouse find your way back to each other.

Part One

FOR BETTER—OR WORSE

How to Identify the
Real Problem in Your Relationship

WHAT IN THE WORLD DID "I DO"?

Marriage may be challenging, but it isn't impossible

What we typically call love is only the start of love.
—ALAIN DE BOTTON, *THE COURSE OF LOVE*

Patrick and I were married early on a Sunday morning. By three that afternoon we were on our way to our honeymoon, driving down the California coast to an idyllic old inn nestled snugly into the Big Sur cliffs. Ignoring our pleas, friends had painted "Just Married" on the back of our car in huge pink and orange Day-Glo letters. People on the freeway honked and smiled, waving their congratulations as we passed. One older couple blew kisses, and a group on motorcycles gave us twenty thumbs-up. Then one particularly assertive motorist, a bearded guy in a red baseball cap, pulled his truck up next to our car. Honking repeatedly, he signaled with his hand for Patrick to roll down his window. He then leaned across the front seat of his truck and, driving beside us at seventy-five miles per hour, shouted out the passenger window, "Dooon't doooo it!"

Everyone has a point of view about marriage. Even before our wedding, I'd noticed how those views tend to be extreme. On one side, we're steeped in all the romantic stuff about finding the one who completes us, having dreams of being utterly, seamlessly, blissfully in love. But there's a bounty of bad press about marriage as well. Jokes and one-liners abound: Marriage isn't a word—*it's a sentence*. Marriage is a wonderful institution—*but who wants to live in an institution*? Marriage is often portrayed as the fast track to unhappiness, with no upside whatever.

As we drove down the coast I thought, surely, there had to be some middle ground between Snow White singing "Someday My Prince Will Come" and the guy in the pickup hoping it wasn't too late for Patrick to ditch me at the altar. I hadn't gone into marriage imagining we'd spend every day walking on sunshine. I saw my expectations as sensible, grown up, down to earth, but not so jaded as to leave out visions of being a couple who still flirts when they're ninety. I believed that I was neither starry-eyed nor cynical, and I was certain that by holding to the rational and sophisticated middle path, I would somehow be safe from the pitfalls that beset others. I knew that Patrick wasn't perfect and neither was I. But we were two caring and intelligent people with the willingness to compromise and work things out. What more could we need?

Right. Not long after my wedding, I began to suspect that my beliefs about marriage were not as sound as I had thought. Most were beliefs I had not articulated or did not know that I held until they proved to be wrong. Things like "If you ask for something nicely, a loving partner will cheerfully do it." Or "Two people with shared values will have nothing to fight about." I assumed that, by definition, marriage turns two separate people into a team—a thriving, happy team. I figured that Patrick and I would face life's inevitable difficulties, but we would face them together. We would know what to do when the going got rough.

Perhaps most naive was the belief that because we loved each other our life together would get better and better with time, no matter what challenges we'd face. Deep down I was sold on the notion that *love will find a way*. Unfortunately, as things between us grew difficult, as we faced problems that we were unprepared to solve, there were many years when love was unable to help either one of us find a way. All that love could do was go into hiding, waiting for some future time when it was safe to come out.

I'd never imagined that we'd argue about things like which brand of soap to buy (and how much to spend on it) or whether it was okay for the kids to eat sweets. We haggled about who was more sleep-deprived, more overworked, and more in need of time off to go to the gym, both of us believing we'd gotten the short end.

Maybe I shouldn't have been so shocked by the reality of marriage; after all, I was and still am a marriage and family therapist. Many of the couples I've seen have been as surprised by their misconceptions about marriage as I'd been about mine. "I knew going into it that marriage takes work. Everyone knows that," one client told me on the eve of her third anniversary. "I'd assumed we'd have our difficulties. But it never occurred to me that my biggest difficulty would be my husband, George!"

Precisely, I thought. I, too, had originally assumed that our biggest challenges would be things outside the marriage, leaving me fully unprepared for what marriage was actually like.

You'd think it would have been obvious, with the divorce rates being what they are, that marriage wouldn't be a walk in the park. You'd think we would have anticipated the rigor of it, recognized that marriage is a long, hard trek along an unfamiliar and sometimes dangerous path.

But we didn't. We set out wearing flip-flops and forgot to bring lunch.

By the time Patrick and I were passing our five-year mark, married life was proving to be more strenuous and infinitely more complicated than we'd ever imagined. We fought more than we laughed, and our fights were always about the same thing. Only that thing was hard to name. What *were* we fighting about, anyway?

That's just it. We didn't fight about anything. We fought about *everything*. Set off by a comment of Patrick's that got under my skin or by a complaint I had about a grease-laden sponge or a pair of shoes left underfoot, our fights would ensnare us in ways we couldn't counter. In the blink of an eye, we'd find ourselves drawn, like hapless bystanders, into the vortex.

"You're never satisfied, are you?"

"Why can't you listen to feedback?"

"What's the big deal?"

"Well, you're the person who started it!"

Not only were our arguments circuitous, exhausting, and about nothing of consequence, they also seemed to gather steam and suck up chance issues in their path like a tornado sweeping across the plains. In the midst of a discussion about bill paying, or whose turn it was to call the babysitter, Patrick would toss in from left field some comment about my "tone" or how, given my behavior, all my therapy training obviously hadn't helped me a nick. I'd say, "Wait, let's stick to the point here," or I might bite the bait and counterattack: "*You're* the one who's being unreasonable, not me," setting off a volley of finger-pointing and rebuttals, grousing and grumbling, blaming and trying to avoid blame, until my mind would go fuzzy and I could no longer think. "What? Wait a minute," I'd mutter. "What are we talking about?" I'd ask, trying to follow what I thought of as his "loopy logic," my IQ points dropping and scattering like pearls unstrung.

"Weren't we talking about your boots on the stairs?" I'd circle back, but by then it was too late. We'd strayed so far afield from whatever had set the stupid thing off that there was no coming back. Once again, we'd ended up in emotional Timbuktu—at which point I was overwhelmed, helpless, and saturated with anxiety.

Over what? Who misplaced the scissors? Whether or not it was I who last unloaded the dishwasher? Those run-ins were my personal definition of hell, and I saw no exit in sight. I kept trying to find the magic words to get Patrick to see how impossible and wrongheaded he was, sincerely believing that if I kept talking (or, to be honest, nagging), he'd finally come around and see things my way.

Without a doubt, we were driving each other around the bend. So much so that I was often convinced I'd married the wrong person, that the whole thing would have been a lot easier and saner with somebody else.

Sometimes I thought that the guy in the truck had been right.

YOU'RE SUCH A GREAT COUPLE— EXCEPT WHEN YOU'RE NOT

With two young kids, a dog, and a marriage that seemed destined to slip off its foundation, I went in search of help, knowing in my heart of hearts that I didn't want to divorce. Having great faith in books, I walked down to my local bookstore, assuming I'd find an abundant collection of useful advice. Unfortunately, much of what I found left me all the more hopeless about myself and my prospects for success. Just perusing the book titles made me fear we were already too far gone: *Embracing the Beloved. Loving Each Other. Getting the Love You Want.* In the midst of one of our typical blowups, *love* was not exactly how I'd describe what I felt.

Standing there in the relationship aisle, I was immediately sad, longing for the time when our feelings of tenderness had been closer at hand. The love that we felt was so often overshadowed by anger and frustration that we were opting to keep our hearts out of reach. If we had to access our love before things could get better, we were definitely sunk. Where was the book called *How to Keep from Killing Your Partner While You Figure Out Why He Drives You Nuts*? I needed that one.

Many books subtly implied that marital strife could be easily corrected. Dozens suggested five or ten or a hundred "simple" things couples can do to be happily married, many of which looked like great ideas for people who were already happy and utterly flimsy for couples like us who were in serious distress. Did the key to happiness truly lie in whether or not we went to sleep naked or slept on the unfamiliar side of the bed? Might we stop squabbling if, as one book suggested, we told the other "You're right" even if we didn't think so? Or perhaps we should come up with pet names for each other, as yet another expert advised, promising that would rekindle the spark. Or maybe, as one popular book touted, we should sleep in separate bedrooms in the hope that we'd soon find each other irresistible. If those strategies were so beneficial to others and so clearly off base for us, was there no help to be found?

Other books made it sound as if marital struggle is an indicator of something having gone terribly wrong: an exception to the rule rather than the rule itself. *Was everyone else effortlessly using I-statements?* I wondered. Were they all being respectful and tolerant, embracing their partner's uniqueness? Why, then, was the divorce rate so high? Obviously, lots of people struggle in their marriage. And some forty percent of them give up. Yet nothing I found explained why. After ninety minutes in the bookstore, the only thing certain was that Patrick and I were perilously close to being one of those statistics.

Clearly a self-help fix wouldn't suffice.

So I set about finding a therapist to help us. Patrick, to his credit, was immediately on board, though I know that spending an hour each week with some stranger, exposing our shortcomings, was not his idea of fun. The woman we chose had been billed as a seasoned couples therapist. *Phew*, I thought, once I'd made our first appointment, perplexed as to why I hadn't taken that step much sooner. Like many struggling couples, Patrick and I had waited until we were utterly miserable before making that first call. We were no doubt in trouble, and, try as I might to figure it out in retrospect, it's not clear to me why we dragged our feet until things got as bad as they did. Had we given up? Were we afraid of what we might uncover? Or were we just too proud to admit how awful things were? At this point it's hard to say.

Still, once we'd finally made it to our first appointment, what we told our therapist spoke volumes about our difficulties. Patrick led with his burning complaints: Winifred is always late, she takes an unbelievable amount of time to get out the door, she wants to stay up later than I do, she complains about things being too messy—that sort of thing. He reeled them off one by one to make sure that the therapist would be clear about what she needed to fix.

I'd heard all of this at least ten thousand times, so I just tuned him out, quietly formulating my answer to the therapist's question "Why are you here?"

When it was my turn, my eyes filled with tears. "I feel as if I'm living in a room with no air," I told her, as she handed me a box of Kleenex. "I feel like a radio . . . you know, with dials and knobs, a volume control, an on-off switch . . . and, it's hard to describe exactly, but it's like my husband wants to control all the dials. The bass and the treble, turning down the volume . . . he *always* wants to turn down the volume." I sighed. "And the problem is I hate it, but I don't know how to get him to stop messing with my dials."

I took a deep breath and leaned back into the plush sofa cushions. *Finally* we were getting some help.

Every Monday night for nearly two years, we brought her the gruesome details of our latest skirmish, our mixed-up mess of *he said / she saids* and *yes, you did / no, I didn'ts*; our infantile behaviors and the dysfunctional responses that followed them. All the while we were hoping that we'd find our way back to being the loving and caring partners we'd been at the outset.

For the first few months, just talking about our struggles relieved some of the pressure. The therapist we'd chosen was a warm, empathic listener who cared a lot about us and about the well-being of our family. Talking with her was a lot like sitting in the living room chatting with a friend—an experience we both found comforting. Some nights we talked more about the kids than our marriage, regaling her with funny anecdotes, getting parenting advice, and sharing the occasional school photograph. Other nights we were so worn out from the previous week's scuffles that we sat slumped in our chairs, too spent for anything but some words of encouragement. The majority of the time, we behaved in her office the way we did at home, the two of us stating our case over and over, trying to convince each other to see things our way. As we went in circles she looked on sympathetically—all the while making suggestions such as "Don't interrupt" or "It's rude to make faces," each of us feeling vindicated when the other was chastised. Sometimes after our sessions we'd continue our fight in the car.

We saw her week after week, believing that by going to therapy we were giving our marriage its best chance of survival, hoping if we kept at it long enough our therapist would eventually figure out what was broken in our relationship and give us instructions about how to repair it. But unfortunately, in the end, she was unable to help us.

"I honestly don't get it," she finally admitted when I asked her point-blank why, nearly two years in, Patrick and I were still fighting like a couple of junkyard dogs. *She didn't get it?* Were we the only couple in her practice unable to resolve conflicts? Were we really that far gone?

"I mean it," she said. "You guys are mostly great together." And she was right. We mostly were. Except when we weren't. And those times were unbearable.

"You guys laugh, you have fun, you have so much in common," she said, almost scratching her head. "It would really be a shame for you to divorce."

True, it *would* be a shame for us to divorce. When I didn't hate Patrick's guts, I loved him dearly. His boyish smile, the tender and patient way he rocked our boys to sleep as infants, his enthusiastic but off-key singing voice, his dogged work ethic. Yet that night, as I sat in our therapist's office with my heart sinking, the possibility of divorce didn't worry me nearly as much as the possibility of continuing to be married and remaining as conflict-obsessed and unhappy as we were.

I couldn't stand the thought of spending the rest of our days going around and around about our trivial grievances.

When our therapist proclaimed us to be "such a great couple," my despair hit a new low. Despite many thousands of dollars spent and scores of hours and effort invested, we were more or less where we'd begun. Except two years more miserable and that much closer to being convinced we were incurable, still facing down a big problem that no one could explain.

With friends around us divorcing and our therapist baffled, obviously nobody had any idea what to do. The implied message was that there's only one way out of a troubled marriage: divorce.

WHEN LOVE ISN'T ENOUGH

Meanwhile, at work, I was faring no better in my attempts to help the couples in my practice who were in the same disheartening situation. Most of them had spent years struggling, too. Some had been told to give up. Many had been given advice that didn't work. Go on a date night. Empathize. Listen more than you speak. One woman, who hadn't had sex with her husband in nearly five years, had been told by her therapist that they should find a nice B and B and spend the weekend in bed. Those couples didn't want to divorce any more than we did, but no one—including me—had a clue what to do.

Frustrated as they were, at least *those* couples had come in together, both of them recognizing that they needed help. Sadder still were the clients who came in alone—frustrated with their relationships but attached to partners who were unwilling to join them in therapy. Those clients felt particularly helpless, and I can't say I blamed them. After all, how could they improve their marriage if their partner didn't have the motivation or commitment to even show up?

The training I'd received years earlier in graduate school provided little guidance. The more traditional psychological literature we'd studied suggested that trouble in marriage is a manifestation of two pathological childhoods blended together to re-create some shadowy and ill-fated pairing that is hard to set right. I'd been taught that marital problems arise from pathology, from sickness in one or both partners, or from dysfunction in the relationship itself. Poor attachment. Childhood trauma. Unhealed wounds. Other texts, similar to those I found in the self-help aisle of my bookstore, made it seem that marital struggle is due to a couple's lack of aptitude at doing something that seems to come naturally to those more skilled, smarter, and luckier in partner choice. Either way, our prognosis was dire.

But rather than give up, I was determined to figure out why.

Like most of the couples I see, I believed I'd tried everything. I'd taken classes, done therapy, and read dozens of books. And though with each failed attempt I grew that much more discouraged, something told me there was more we could do. Something said that regardless of our past or our parents, no matter how difficult we found each other to be, no matter how often (and fiercely) we fought, we could learn to do better.

We could change. Even if I had no idea what that would look like or how we would do it, I had a hunch that there was some secret door we could pass through, some stone left unturned.

Maybe our saving grace was that Patrick and I are both stubborn by nature and we'd rather die trying than fail at something we've attempted. Maybe my curiosity about why marriage is hard for so many of us drove me not to give up. Or perhaps we were like the old couple in the joke who were asked about their secret to sustaining a seventy-five-year marriage. The answer: We never wanted to get a divorce on the same day.

Fortunately, that was true for us. Despite nights spent with our backs to each other, days barely speaking, and a number of anniversaries celebrated with minimal enthusiasm (including one that we chose to ignore), neither one of us ever made a convincing stand for divorce. Instead, we opted to stay put. If it was not one, it was the other of us who maintained some flicker of hope, extending a hand, talking the other back from the ledge. Seemingly against all odds. Unlike many of our friends. Flying in the face of allegedly credible evidence that we were destined to fail. We both kept two feet in, and I'm glad that we did.

As for my newlywed notion about love finding a way—I didn't realize it at the time, but love ended up playing a steadying role. Even though at times it seemed reduced to barely an ember, our love never died. No matter how deeply entrenched we might be, every Sunday at nine we'd climb into bed together and watch *Masterpiece Theater*. We couldn't resist smiling if I said "You lost your shoe," an inside joke that was ours alone.

We were likely to reconcile if one of us needed help finding our glasses or making a plane reservation. And nothing could stop us from being there for our children. Once in a while we said "I love you" and meant it.

But love alone wasn't enough. Love needed some high-level assistance before it was too late. Love needed someone to point the way, to explain why we were driving each other crazy and what we could do about it. Without that help, we truly were doomed. And then, thank goodness, help finally arrived.

Like love itself, it came when I least expected it and in a way I had never imagined.

2

WHY MARRIAGE CAN BE SO HARD

We're playing a game,
and we don't even understand the rules

---

*In every marriage more than a week old, there are
grounds for divorce. The trick is to find, and continue to
find, the grounds for marriage.*

—ROBERT ANDERSON, *SOLITAIRE/DOUBLE SOLITAIRE*

I was just locking up my office one evening when I saw the red light on my answering machine start to blink. *Ugh*, I groaned, dreading the possibility that it was something urgent. It had been a particularly long and difficult day, with one couple threatening to divorce over the unresolved issue of which preschool to choose and another bringing in a cassette tape of their fight, wanting to replay it so that I could take sides. *Why bother with a tape?* I'd wondered, since they'd resumed in my office the fight they'd started at home.

Most couples' fights are as idiotic and unresolvable as the fights I had with Patrick—about the fastest route to the theater, the proper place to store olive oil, or, as in the fight that Bruce and Cindy had recorded on tape, whose turn it was to shampoo the dog. But when it came to arguing, Bruce and Cindy made Patrick and me look like a couple of lightweights, the two of them battling so fiercely that I was stunned at the intensity. When they fought, which they did regularly, Bruce's face would turn beet red, and I feared that one day he would have a stroke right there in my office.

They were, without a doubt, my couple from hell. Every day of their marriage offered new opportunities for the two of them to torture each other. And once a week they tortured me. Some days they were into it before I'd opened the door. "*Listen* to me!" I once heard Cindy shout as she came down the walkway. "No, you listen to me!" came Bruce's reply. "*No. You* listen to *me*," she came back louder and more urgently. "*No!*" they insisted simultaneously, both of them imploring the other to listen but neither of them capable of anything that resembled the listening they craved.

The first time I saw them, I was unable to get a word in edgewise, let alone formulate a constructive thought about how I might help:

"I never said that!"

"Yes, you did."

"I did not!"

"You're unbelievable!"

"Are you calling me a liar?"

Trying to break into the action was like stepping in front of a buffalo stampede. Words were of no use whatsoever, so after several futile attempts—*Cindy? Bruce? Hello?*—I was finally able to get their attention by wildly waving my arms, my presence seeming to startle them as if I'd suddenly dropped in through the ceiling. Sometimes the only way to keep my

thoughts straight around them was to get up, stand braced behind my big leather chair, and address them from a distance,
like a bank teller safe behind an inch-thick wall of glass.

That night's session was, by comparison, calmer than most,
as Bruce made the unprecedented move of saying that perhaps
he'd made too big a deal over nothing. Even so, by the time it
was over, I was worn out and hungry, looking forward to a quiet
evening at home. Patrick and I had talked about spending the
weekend with friends at their beach house, which, after a day
like I'd had, couldn't come a minute too soon.

Though some weeks were more challenging than others,
most weeks left me wishing there was more I could do. Hearing
the tedious details of who'd said what to whom or who was at
fault frequently left me thinking that there had to be more ways
to help my couples than make gestures of sympathy or brainstorm with them about ways they might compromise.

Much to my relief, when I pressed PLAY, the message on my
machine was from a colleague, suggesting that the two of us
sign up for a training class.

"This one might be worth doing," she said, "but it's two full
days, this coming Friday and Saturday."

"Saturday, too?" I lamented out loud, seeing my weekend
plans wither away. It was hard to imagine that anything could
be worth skipping the beach.

The workshop was called "Love Under Pressure: Surviving
and Thriving with Your Difficult Couples." My friend read high-
lights from the brochure:

"'Dr. Ellyn Bader of the Couples Institute in Menlo Park . . .

advanced theoretical material . . . increase your own personal strengths . . . best possible results with hostile/angry, borderline, narcissistic, and passive-aggressive partners. Videotapes and clinical case examples. Twelve units of continuing education.'

"If you've got any difficult couples," my friend said with a chuckle, "give me a call."

Did I have any difficult couples? What other kind are there? Some of my couples had run through four or five therapists before me, and a few had been fired by therapists who had finally thrown up their hands. Every couple I saw challenged me in their unique way—and doing therapy with them left me wondering, at times, if I might have been happier being a tree pruner.

"I may have a difficult couple or two," I joked with my friend when I called to reply. "Or three," I threw in, "if you count Patrick and me!"

After a shared laugh and some discussion of logistics, I reluctantly agreed. "Okay, fine," I said. Waste of time or not, I needed the twelve units of continuing education.

GROWING SEPARATELY, TOGETHER: A REVOLUTIONARY IDEA

Bright and early that Friday, we were on the road, stopping only for tea and a couple of muffins before heading into rush hour traffic. By nine a.m., we were seated in a pair of stiff blue chairs in a gaudy hotel ballroom that was already freezing from air-conditioning. It was a room of mostly women. *Where are the men?* I wondered. Do they all opt out of the scut work of doing therapy with couples?

At each seat was a packet filled with charts and questionnaires, a lengthy set of definitions, and what looked at first glance like a lot of gimmicks: seemingly facile instructions on the etiquette of listening and a handful of quick-fix exercises to offer our couples. I thought immediately of Bruce and Cindy. They were the main reason I'd signed up in the first place: to learn how to thrive and survive with *them*. Could anything this simplistic help with problems like theirs?

I thought about the time they'd taken a road trip up into Canada and things had escalated to biting and scratching. Cindy had ended up leaping from the car in near-freezing temperatures without grabbing her coat. Bruce had driven away and left her standing there for nearly three and a half hours. And the time Cindy had given several boxes of Bruce's books to Goodwill because he refused to get new bookshelves. Try as I might to get them to be civil—let alone nice—to each other, nothing I did made even a dent. Then I came to the quote on page two of the workshop syllabus:

Central to the advancement of human civilization is the spirit of open inquiry. We must not only learn to tolerate our differences—we must welcome them as the richness and diversity which can lead to true intelligence.

—Albert Einstein

I tried to picture die-hard vegan Bruce welcoming Cindy's desire to eat a hamburger as rich and diverse as when he wouldn't even wear leather shoes. I couldn't imagine him embracing her desire to do anything, for that matter, unless *he* endorsed it. I flipped through the workshop materials and began to regret that I'd come.

The workshop was an introduction to the Bader-Pearson Developmental Model of Couples Therapy. *Individual* development was a concept with which I was quite familiar, but the course leader, Dr. Ellyn Bader, was going to give us a two-day deep dive into the meaning and implications of development as it applied to *couples*. For the first hour, Dr. Bader, a gentle, seemingly reserved, and obviously knowledgeable woman, spoke to us about the normal and natural stages of development that occur in every couple's relationship. Couples develop much the way children do, she explained, beginning in a state where there is little separateness and moving toward a more developed separate self and a greater self-sufficiency.

Ellyn showed a series of slides that illustrated how couples move from the blissful, merged state of courtship into an unavoidable period of turbulence, as their *isn't-it-amazing-how-much-we're-alike* feeling gives way to a painful awareness of the ways they are different. If couples can learn to tolerate the tension that naturally comes as they struggle with those differences—if they can grow to accept that their likes and desires often diverge, that they see and interpret the world differently, that, like it or not, they don't always want the same things—what lies ahead is far more satisfying and sustainable than the initial bond that was based solely on *we-ness*. Partners who have done the internal growing that those early stages require become genuinely curious about how the other partner sees things, secure enough in themselves to no longer find their differences threatening. The reward, Ellyn said, is a relationship of vitality and mutual respect, a true partnership that holds the capacity for profound intimacy.

These are the developmental stages Ellyn laid out:[1]

1. *Symbiosis:* The "honeymoon phase," when you're so in love and so close that you can't imagine ever *not* seeing eye to eye. We've all been there, and it's delightful—but it never lasts.

2. *Differentiation:* The next stage of development, when couples start to see what's distinct about each of them (and often struggle mightily to resolve or eradicate those differences). This is where I often meet my clients, and it's the stage I realized I was mired in with Patrick—and had been for years.

3. *Exploration:* The development of separate selves. This is the stage when a couple starts to explore their own interests and needs, independent of each other. It's a scary stage for many, because often they worry that if they're not growing together, they are growing apart. In reality, the opposite is true.

4. *Rapprochement:* When couples feel secure enough in their separateness, accepting enough of their differences, that they long for a deeper connection with each other and begin to "turn towards."

5. *Synergy:* The stage that allows for that deeper, more intimate connection, as couples know that they're loved as they are, that they no longer need to hide the potentially "unacceptable" parts of themselves the way they did early on. At this stage, independence and interdependence easily coexist.

In the coming hours (and the coming years, in my ongoing training and in my own marriage) I'd be learning a lot more about these different stages. But just knowing that they even existed was eye-opening. For the first time ever, the winding and often bumpy road of marriage made sense.

Ellyn then made it clear that progressing through these stages was no simple process; that couples don't easily sail from level to level and arrive at some mythic relationship nirvana. All that growing takes work, *hard* work—with most of it taking place inside each individual partner.

Inside the individual partner? *Really?* And did Ellyn really mean *most*? I had assumed that the hard work was *between* partners, working on things such as tone of voice, eye rolling, and who said what in an argument. Apparently the approach I'd been taking was missing the point.

FALLING IN LOVE VERSUS LOVE

Like children growing into adulthood, Ellyn explained, couples grow by facing the unfamiliar, acquiring new skills, gaining competency, managing tasks of greater and greater complexity, noting that this process of growth is designed to continue over a lifetime. No stage can be skipped, Ellyn stressed, because the experience a couple gains and the abilities they acquire in each stage provide the foundation for the developmental work of the stages that follow. It's like climbing a ladder, I thought, couples ascending from one stage to the next, carrying their new skills and capacities with them as they work their way to the top.

Ellyn also seemed to be saying that couples don't grow hand in hand. One may move ahead while the other hangs back. Though you can't force your partner to grow, you can start growing on your own. Once *you* start the work, your changes will influence both your partner and your marriage as a whole. Often—though not always—your partner will follow.

For many people, the trip up the developmental ladder is not easy or smooth. Some lack the strength and stamina they need to master what each stage demands, while others get stalled, clinging desperately to the lower rungs of the ladder, afraid to face what is difficult or unknown about the stages ahead. Growth and change take resilience, even fearlessness, Ellyn said—qualities that, as therapists, we need to encourage.

Ellyn went on to talk about the anxiety that accompanies change, how people back away from change when it threatens their sense of security, and how anxiety tolerance is a necessary step toward a deeper intimacy and fuller sexuality. Intimacy requires that we take risks, she explained, and I thought about how guarded so many of my couples are, wanting greater closeness but afraid to open up.

I thought about myself, about Patrick, and about how guarded *we* were and how shockingly far we were from this kind of ideal "separate and together" relationship that tolerated differences rather than resisted them. Ellyn said that being curious and open—not threatened by difference but willing to embrace it—was an essential ingredient in a healthy relationship. Unfortunately, those were skills that neither Patrick nor I had yet acquired.

What would it be like, I wondered, to be open-minded and accepting about Patrick playing Willie Nelson in the car while we're out doing errands? And, more challenging still, when he was singing along? What if he didn't disparage the way I sometimes liked to do nothing, sitting in the back garden just watching the sky? From the way Ellyn had talked about the hard work it entails, I had a feeling that there was a lot more to tolerating difference than one might get at first glance—more, I figured, than being broad-minded enough to live with the toothpaste squeezed from the top.

Ellyn stepped down from the podium and moved toward the group. "How many of you remember what it's like to fall in love?" she asked, and every hand went up. "You meet someone, they're perfect, you fall in love, right?"

Falling in love was like walking into a surprise party: unexpected, delightful, and a bit disconcerting. The day Patrick and I met, I was going to a job interview and he was headed to work, both of us waiting to catch the same streetcar. In a matter of weeks we went from strangers to friends, and then the next thing I knew I was wondering whether one of our children might be a freckle-faced redhead.

Falling in love meant that for every sane and rational minute there were five spent thinking about the way Patrick stirred his tea counterclockwise or how his left eyebrow formed a little V before he said something serious or how utterly masterful he was at folding the newspaper. It meant dropping my keys down a storm drain and showing up at a Friday-morning job interview on Thursday—and not really caring about either mistake. After our first night together I was so lost in the clouds that I sailed right through a stop sign and crashed my roommate's car sidelong into a taxicab.

Hasn't everyone been there? This is the way most relationships begin: the honeymoon phase, where all that matters is that we've found someone so right. Ellyn referred to this first stage of development as *symbiosis*, or the *symbiotic stage*,[*] emphasizing the temporary loss of self and the merging of lives that occurs as the couple forms their initial, and hopefully enduring, attachment.[2] Like babies when they first attach to their mothers, they form an all-encompassing bond with someone ideal and all-powerful with whom they feel unequivocally safe from harm.

In couples, symbiosis is the phase of infatuation and enchantment, where two become one, where *we-ness* predominates over *I-ness* and difference takes a backseat as we drive through the wondrous landscape of togetherness.

But love's intoxication lasts only so long. Always, without exception, the honeymoon ends. We notice, for the first time,

---

[*] Based on Margaret Mahler's stages of infant development.

some disconcerting trait or a behavior that we really don't like. The way he curses when frustrated. The way she needs to be right. How she's spiteful or careless. How he leaves the toilet seat up. This *first disillusionment*, the term Ellyn used, marks the first challenge a couple faces together, a challenge that will be either a turning point that leads to growth and deepening or a deal breaker that tips things over irreparably. For most couples, this disillusionment is felt as a crisis—the first glimpse of a future that will forever include the not-so-appealing things about their once perfect partner. A future where there's no longer just a harmonious *we* but two distinct *I*s as well.

If a couple's first go at grappling with difference goes badly, as it so often does, many use this failed experience as a reason to avoid future risk. Some distance themselves, while others hide their true feelings, vowing never to reveal difference again, or at least not anytime soon. Many do both.

This risk avoidance virtually guarantees that they'll be stuck at the bottom of the developmental ladder with no idea why they can't get unstuck.

YOUR FIRST DISILLUSIONMENT
TELLS A VALUABLE STORY

Ellyn had been speaking for ninety minutes or so when she asked us to put down our pens and shift the focus from our clients to ourselves.

"What was the first disillusionment you experienced with

your partner?" she asked, reminding us that the first disillusionment is quite often the first place a couple gets stuck.

My answer came instantly. I knew precisely the incident she was asking us to recall. I remembered it so vividly, I could see the dust motes in the afternoon sunlight in front of my San Francisco apartment and hear the very tone of the words Patrick and I spoke. We'd known each other six weeks, tops.

"What happened?" she asked. "How did you handle it?"

How *did* I handle my first disillusionment? I asked myself.

We were still in the early weeks of infatuation, when our every moment together confirmed, without a doubt, that we were perfectly matched. We read the same books, we both liked to cook, I thought his jokes were funny (and he thought the same about mine), and the two of us could talk for hours on end and never get bored. Better still, we were curious about the deeper questions in life, open-minded about life's possibilities: open to growth.

Then one afternoon, I asked Patrick to give me one last kiss before he left. We'd said good-bye, he was already on his bicycle, just setting off for his evening shift at the restaurant where he worked. He'd put the Velcro strap around his pant leg, along with the safety light that flashed on his backpack, and was just about to go. As he turned to wave good-bye, I reached for him. "One more," I said, tugging coquettishly at the nubby sleeve of his sweater. I figured he'd be tickled by my invitation, by my refusal to let him go, by my flirtation. *Of course* he'd want one more kiss. Who wouldn't? Who wouldn't want a dozen? But he hesitated, the little place between his eyebrows tightening for a moment, his head turned just slightly away. So I stepped back.

"Bye," he said with a half-smile as he pushed off from the curb and was gone.

The next time I saw him, a day or two later, I suggested that we talk. "What was that about?" I inquired, certain he'd be more than happy to explore this with me. We were, after all, open to inquiry, curious: interested in what things mean.

"It was too much," he said matter-of-factly. "I needed to go."

From his point of view, I'd asked for too much, for more than he wanted to give. *But too much of what?* I wondered. Had I been wrong to want him or just wrong to ask? Or had it been the tug on his sleeve or the come-hither look in my eye? Was that what had scared him? *Hmmm*, I brooded. *Since when was he such a choirboy?*

Or was it something else? Was I being needy or clingy, or had I just not taken it well, being turned down? Was he, in fact, saying it was I: that *I* was too much? With that, I felt hurt, and then, very quickly, I was mired in self-doubt.

Patrick and I went back and forth a few times, always coming to the same stuck place: *Hadn't I given you enough already?* up against *What's wrong with asking?* Then I decided to drop it. I was twenty-two and in love, and besides, I figured, it was probably nothing.

Sitting there in the workshop, I was utterly stunned. Just remembering what had happened still conjured the sharp sting of loss, reignited the old embers of hurt and anger, as if it were happening right then. It had been nearly twenty years, yet, there in the room, I was choking back tears and my hands were clammy with sweat.

Then Ellyn asked, "What can you learn about yourself from the experience you had?"

Learn from it? I'd known all along the details of what had gone on, but I'd never thought to ask what I might learn. What *did* that first fight say about me?

First off, it told me that I could sure hold a grudge! Twenty years later, and I still felt wronged. I gulped. Patrick had been trying to point out my grudge holding for years, but I'd always denied it. Next it said that when faced with my new boyfriend seeing things in a way that was wildly different from how I saw them, I had simply given up. Sure, I had fussed a bit, but then I had backed off. But I'd never forgotten the incident, and I'd not let it go.

I questioned, for the first time, why I had gone silent; why, despite being as upset as I was, I'd chosen to minimize its importance, to tell myself it was nothing. I'd never before realized that the choice had been mine. Yes, Patrick had pushed back, but *I* was the one who had given up at that point. *I* had given up, and for all these years I'd blamed *my* giving up on *him*.

"Oh," I heard myself say out loud. Maybe I'm not as strong as I thought.

Maybe the change I'd been seeking was more about *me* than *us*.

With that I was no longer focused on Bruce and Cindy or any of the other difficult couples in my practice. Not the couple crushed by the betrayal of an affair. Not the guy with the hair-trigger temper or the woman who couldn't get the kids to school on time or the newlyweds who already thought they should divorce. As I thought about all that Ellyn was saying—about partners seeing their own part in creating their difficulties, about difference potentially being a catalyst for growth—something began to happen inside me. Something quiet and powerful, but I had no idea what. My whole body felt sweaty and cold at the same time, and my heart started to race. I thought of people caught in a riptide, pulled out to sea. Suddenly deep in, the sand rushing out from under them. Don't fight the waves, they say. Let the current take you, or you'll drown.

By the time we finally spilled out into the sun-drenched lobby for our first break in nearly two hours, I'd figured it out. My friend and I picked up a couple of small plastic water bottles and headed outside.

"I'm in trouble," I muttered as we settled ourselves on a bench.

"What do you mean?" she asked, quickly looking around, as if maybe I'd forgotten my purse, or someone I didn't want to see had shown up.

"I mean that if what Ellyn's saying is true—if Patrick and I are as underdeveloped as it sounds—well, honestly, I feel totally floored." From her nod, it seemed that she had had similar thoughts about herself.

Was I overreacting, I wondered, believing that my relationship was still in its infancy, nearly two decades in? Did I truly not know a thing about what really makes marriage work? Maybe I was going overboard thinking I had to now remake myself from the ground up. Then again, maybe that was precisely what I needed to do.

"Maybe we're like med students who are convinced they've got every single sickness they're learning about," I said, half-heartedly scrambling for a way out.

We looked at each other for about ten seconds, hoping one of us would think the med student analogy would stick. But unfortunately, it didn't hold true for either of us.

IT STARTS WITH ME—BUT WHERE DO I BEGIN?

Two hours down and ten to go. Back in my seat, I felt sick and astonished. But mostly sick. *What am I going to do?* I kept asking myself. What if Patrick and I are as immature as I thought? What happens then? What if we're too far behind to grow up, permanently stuck in preschool, still throwing sand?

"It's perfectly normal," Ellyn explained. Lots of couples stall out in the early stages of development and need help getting unstuck. *Normal? Really?* It's *normal* to feel as if you have no voice? It's *normal* for your head to spin or for you to feel like giving up before you've even tried? How can it be *normal* for two people to act like children for decades?

How many of the other professionals in that room were unable to take a solid stand with their mate about something important? I wondered. How many of them gave up the way I apparently did? I came to learn much later that the answer is *most*. Most of us struggle when our viewpoint is challenged, especially by someone who is very important to us, someone whose opinion seems crucial—someone such as our spouse. Sure, we might yell or stamp our feet; some of us might cry; but an actual stand, where we plant our feet, where we define ourselves and courageously face whatever response we're given? Where we don't capitulate in the face of our differences, feel persecuted, or think we have to get a divorce? It takes strength to be clearheaded and steady when our partners disagree or push back, when they criticize us, when they want us to change. Though all along I'd thought of myself as competent and strong, it was becoming more and more evident that when it was time to come toe-to-toe with the serious issues in my marriage, I had the staying power of a dandelion.

I considered again how, despite seeming bold, I too often capitulated, shouting and flailing my arms, mistakenly thinking that fighting meant I was "standing up for myself." Maybe the way I blindly stuck to my guns wasn't about strength at all. Maybe I was, in fact, lacking in backbone, seemingly strong and competent on the outside but more like a kid on the inside, wanting safety and approval, despite its high cost.

As I took in what Ellyn was saying, I began to question much of what I'd thought true about Patrick and me as well. We'd picked each other for the things we had in common, for the ways we agreed, for the ways we worked well as a team, only now our high need for consensus was driving both of us nuts. We *were* different—often dramatically so. But, finding a way to accept our differences, to—what did Einstein's quote say—*welcome* them? For Patrick and me, that seemed close to impossible. How could I possibly welcome Patrick's three-day-old coffee cup left to mold in my car or the way he'd pressure me in January to get to work on the taxes? Might the day ever come when he would welcome the way I rewashed the dishes after he was done?

That's precisely the point of Stage Two, Ellyn said. *Differentiation*: the stage of development when couples struggle with difference; when they use that struggle to more clearly define themselves and help them grow up—the very thing that Patrick and I had failed to accomplish.

This is the stage that requires couples to venture beyond the safety of sameness and begin to take risks, to reveal thoughts and desires that often highlight the differences between them: *I don't really like opera. I'm more into football. I'd rather have sex with the lights on. I'm not turned on by your kiss.* As more and more of the temporarily suspended *I-ness* re-emerges, most couples find themselves in distress. What happened to the blissful days when all things went smoothly, when they had so much in common; the time before difference turned their world upside down? When couples are unable to sustain the idyllic sameness they experienced in courtship, some call into question the entire relationship, fearing, for the first time, that they've made a mistake. "What have I gotten myself into?" they ask, having no idea that, quite likely, nothing is wrong.

Some couples are able to rise to the challenge of what Stage Two demands by developing healthy ways to handle the tension of their differences, instead of shying away from them. Through practice, they learn to advocate for themselves and effectively manage their conflicts. When faced with the anxiety of standing separate from their partner, they learn to calm themselves down, trusting that there's a way to take good care of themselves while still caring about the other, trusting that the relationship can handle some bumps.

Growth takes place inside and out: *inside* ourselves as we strive to develop a solid and well-defined sense of ourselves; and *outside*, in our relationship, as we grow increasingly able to be solidly and securely connected both to our partner and to our own beliefs and desires. If you aren't strengthening and defining yourself as an individual, you don't stand a chance of growing and developing as a strong, healthy couple. This two-level process of growth goes on throughout our lifetime as a couple, as we face the inevitable and unknown challenges that come our way.

More often than not, struggling couples are struggling because of how challenging it is to find their way through Stage Two. Those who cannot will approach their crisis in one of two unhealthy ways: either they'll be caught in repeating cycles of conflict, or they'll aim to avoid conflict at all costs by minimizing their differences or denying they exist. Whether fighting or fleeing, both strategies are ineffective and are, ironically, geared toward the same end: to return to the experience of safety and sameness that the couple had in Stage One—which, as it turns out, is a fruitless endeavor.

Most of my practice consists of couples who have gotten bogged down in Stage Two. Many are unable to tolerate the anxiety of being contradicted or challenged; few can take a stand without wobbling or backtracking. Most lack the psychological wherewithal to hold fast to their convictions when their partner is pressuring them to capitulate or conform. And almost all of them fear that the appearance of difference might mark the beginning of the end, that if not turned back into sameness, the differences between them will blow the relationship apart. (And sometimes it does.)

Throughout the day Ellyn drove this point home: that though most of us wish to, we cannot go back. The work, she stressed, is for a couple to move forward: to become sturdy and resilient in the face of interpersonal difficulty, to learn to tolerate painful emotions without shutting down, attacking, or being wiped out. All of which requires that we step well beyond the bounds of our comfort zone. It requires that we risk.

Without this there is no growth. Period.

"Okay," I said. "If that's what it takes," having little idea what I had just committed to doing.

From there I was headed for places I had never imagined. And I was determined to drag my marriage along with me.

Ellyn had opened a door, and I had walked through.

THE FIRST STEP IN A LONG JOURNEY

At nine the next morning, I, and the other ninety-nine therapists who were hoping to thrive and survive as I was, filed once again into the now too-warm conference room with our notepads and coffee, our ergonomic pillows and our extra sweaters, should we need them later—all of us eager to get started on the "how to" part of doing therapy with the difficult couples who had most of us stymied.

Before things got under way, I watched Ellyn walk back and forth, move her water glass, gather her papers, clip on her microphone, chat with her husband, Peter Pearson, the codirector of their institute. *What kind of marriage do they have?* I wondered. We'd talked on the first day about differentiation: the degree to which a person can maintain a solid, separate, and resilient self around a highly important person, such as one's spouse. Could Ellyn do that? Or did she want to tear her hair out in frustration when she tried to solve problems with Pete? What would she do if Pete left tomato seeds all over the cutting board?

Ellyn had opened the previous day's session with a joke about standing at the rim of the Grand Canyon with Pete, how in times past they'd have had second thoughts about hiking so near the edge. Something about finally trusting that he wouldn't push her over. Or she him? I didn't quite get it at first, and in fact it was unsettling to hear the teacher admit she had feelings like that. But by the end of day two I realized Ellyn was saying that marriage is difficult for all of us, even the experts. These hot-tempered feelings—they're something most of us feel.

Over and over, she used the word *normal* to describe the kinds of cockeyed scenarios that Patrick and I often played out—the very ones that left me convinced we were doomed. The circuitous fighting, the insufferable stalemates, the blaming and capitulating, the sense of defeat. For the first time in ages, I found myself thinking that despite our problems, maybe there was hope. Even if we were on the more messed-up end of normal, that at least placed us somewhere on the curve. It was so reassuring to hear about the difficulties that she and Pete had faced, for her to "admit" that they'd wanted to murder each other, to joke about it. To laugh.

Of course we struggle with our partners. Of course we're frustrated at times.

Relationships are hard!

I now make a point of saying those exact words in the very first session I have with a new couple. "Relationships are challenging for everyone," I say, making it clear when I say it that I'm including my own. Unlike the disconcerting message Patrick and I got from our first couples therapist that our discord was "puzzling" and might lead to divorce, I tell couples that struggling in their marriage is both normal and valuable. Frustration is unavoidable, given our inevitable differences. Trying to work out a satisfying life with another person is a complicated job, and without proper tools, that job can seem impossible. Most couples have the same look of relief I had when I first heard this from Ellyn, reassured, as I was, that we're all in the same boat.

To be fair, until I attended my first workshop with Ellyn, I knew as little as our first therapist about helping couples like us. Every couple, no matter their issues, presented me with challenges that I could not effectively address. My most difficult couples ran circles around me while I experienced myself as a dazed bystander, at best. But even with my run-of-the-mill couples in trouble, my limited skill set kept me from making any meaningful impact. Most days I felt frustrated, stuck treading water when I wanted to move forward, feeling clearly outnumbered by two people who were better at doing their thing than I was at interrupting it.

Now I actually knew what to do. Yes, I was at best a beginner, but with this new set of ideas and practical tools (plus an entire yellow legal pad of notes to refer to), I felt confident that the work I would do with my couples would actually help them. In many ways, the material was simple and straightforward, and though I had plenty to learn, I felt ready to go.

Except for one thing: the therapeutic interventions that Pete and Ellyn modeled were far more daring than any I had ever encountered. Like when Pete said he had reprints of an article about passive-aggressive men that he'd pull out of his filing cabinet and hand to any client for whom it seemed fit. "Read this, and let me know if it sounds like you," he'd say calmly. Or how, in a role play, Ellyn leaned forward and confronted the husband who was sidestepping his wife's concern about how he flirts with other women. "You keep changing the subject," she said firmly. "I'm wondering if you'd be willing to stick with what your wife is addressing?"

At the time those interventions seemed so direct, so in-your-face. *Can a therapist really get away with things like that?* I wondered, having little idea that in time I'd be making moves as bold—or bolder.

Then there was the way Ellyn responded to the woman whose husband claimed he'd lost interest in sex because she'd gotten too fat. While the woman was sobbing, Ellyn faced her and said, "Do you know this isn't about *you*? Do you know this is about *your husband, Frank*?" she pressed. "It's about the template he has in his mind about sexual beauty."

"You would *say* that?" I asked Ellyn when we had a moment alone.

"Of course I would," she said matter-of-factly. "You can't help your clients unless you challenge them. That's your job." She smiled, placing a reassuring hand on my shoulder.

It's my job to challenge people. It's my job to push for change. The basic message was to keep the heat on the difficult issues, look for self-deceptions and inconsistencies, and ask the client to self-reflect: "You're saying x, but you're doing y." Don't let your clients back you off the important issues. The goal is to move a stuck couple further up the developmental ladder, to initiate growth. That would require something greater than words of encouragement or hand-holding. In order to make the kinds of interventions Pete and Ellyn advised, I was going to have to ramp up my audacity.

And to do that, I would have to be someone I had not yet become.

During the break, I wandered the lobby alone, taking in the waning afternoon light, the bustling throng of therapists buying lattes from a brass cart just outside the front door. The workshop would be over in just a few hours. And my questions far outnumbered my answers.

While Ellyn gave her closing remarks, I thought only of what lay ahead for me—in my work with clients, in my marriage, and in the already shifting ways in which I saw myself. Everything was about to change. It *had* to change. But how? By doing what?

Ellyn's words played in my head: It's deadly to compromise the core parts of yourself. The work of therapy is to build greater emotional capacity and resiliency. You have to go against your natural instinct for self-preservation if you want to grow. You'll have to take risks.

There I was again, pulled out to sea, awash in a riptide. No foothold. No bearings. Trying to calm myself. Hoping not to drown.

What now? I asked myself, nearly breathless, my pulse pounding loud in my ears. All around me people gathered up their notebooks and water bottles, none of them panicking, gasping for air. I closed my eyes, inhaling slowly and then breathing out until my heart rate finally slowed down. The workshop was over, and it was clear that Ellyn wasn't going to hand me a map or a developmental road atlas with the best travel route highlighted in red. *What now?* I repeated, unable to recognize until I'd calmed down that Ellyn had, in fact, given me what I needed the most.

No matter how scared I was, no matter how uncharted the road ahead, at least I'd gained a sense of the territory. At least I could now look at the map of marriage and locate the little arrow that said: YOU ARE HERE. No matter that Patrick and I had been stuck there for years, haplessly wandering its dark and shadowy nether regions. So what if we'd have to work hard to get out?

For the first time in years I had a feeling of hope. Though

we'd spent sixteen years constructing the mess we were in, I finally knew what had gotten us there, and I knew at least some of what would get us out. With what I'd learned that weekend, we'd gone from *lost cause* to *lost*. And that was a vast improvement. After all, I reassured myself, lost can be found.

The Takeaway:
Why Marriage Can Be So Hard

- All relationships are hard, not just yours.

- Your differences are not going to go away. You can struggle with them endlessly, or you can strive to tolerate and even embrace them.

- All relationship work begins inside you.

3

DON'T BE AFRAID TO CHANGE FIRST

How to become the front-runner for change in your marriage

———————

To dare is to lose one's footing momentarily.
To not dare is to lose oneself.
—SØREN KIERKEGAARD

Amid all the uncertainty that the workshop had generated, I was sure about one thing: ready or not, there were big changes ahead—at work, in my marriage, and inside myself. I'd been emboldened by Pete and Ellyn's loud and clear message: Challenge yourself. Approach your difficulties with courage. Be willing to take risks.

Given the state of my marriage, I was willing to do almost anything to get us out of our rut. But on a gut level, Pete and Ellyn's directive to "step outside my comfort zone" seemed like an invitation to step off a cliff. I imagined making new moves, ranging from something as simple as asking Patrick to clean up his breakfast dishes instead of leaving them for me to proposing we buy more life insurance to sharing my ideas about how to spice up our sex life. But all I could envision was Patrick rolling his eyes, scoffing, or worse, telling me that what I wanted was frivolous and unnecessary, that all I did was complain. And there we'd be again, back at our original scene of the crime, our first disillusionment fight, where I was asking for more and once again he was telling me that I was asking for too much.

That night, driving home from the workshop, my mind was wild with a chorus of contradictory voices:

You can do this was immediately met with *Who are you kidding?*

Then came *How hard can it be? You have plenty of strength*, quickly followed by *Don't kid yourself, it's a suicide mission.*

Back and forth they argued, one voice rationally encouraging me to rise to the challenge: *Listen, this isn't the first difficult task you've faced in your life, and it likely won't be the last*, while a more frantic one came up with a dozen reasons not to even get started.

As I turned onto our street, I was left with one nagging concern:

Have I lost my mind?

What if I'd overestimated my strength? What if Patrick was too formidable a foe? What if I leapt into the great unknown and discovered that despite that tiny, glowing ember of hope, we were inherently doomed?

I'd heard plenty of other couples say the same thing: What if we're too different? Too broken? Maybe our struggles are a sign that we should give up. "You're the expert," they'd said. "What are our odds?"

Calm down, I told myself as I put my key in the door. *It will be fine.* I'd been gone a mere thirty-six hours, and though I'd begun to change in small ways already, there was no need to panic. My marriage was the same as I'd left it when I'd driven off on Friday. A marriage that included both the wonderful and the woefully messed up, as it had all along.

Stepping into the house, I knew that Patrick would, as usual, be genuinely glad to see me. The boys would be kicking a soccer ball in the backyard or watching TV. The table would be set, and within minutes of my arrival the dinner they'd cooked would be brought to the table. Though my long-term plan for my marriage was certainly daunting, my immediate one was to sit down to eat and catch up on all that I'd missed. After that I'd take a hot bath and begin thinking about where to begin.

Whatever else we might do, I was clear that Patrick and I needed to grow up. Buried under our childish ways was a set of strengths waiting to be unearthed, and I was prepared to start digging. *It's never too late*, I repeated, certain we could make some headway toward acting like the adults that we (chronologically) were. Though my real training as a couples therapist had just begun, I'd learned enough to know this: when you're stuck at the bottom of the developmental ladder, the way out is up.

KNOWING JUST ENOUGH TO BE DANGEROUS

My first postworkshop weeks in the office were both exciting and humbling. I was having more fun at work than I'd had in years. Heeding Ellyn's command to take risks and be bold, I was making statements and asking questions that had previously seemed way out of bounds. Such as "What did you tell yourself that made it okay to repeatedly lie?" Or "I'm going to say something you don't want to hear. Are you ready?" I delighted in seeing my clients look more deeply and thoughtfully at themselves, most of them working harder in therapy than ever before. But there were also times I froze up, straining to come up with a question or comment that would have an impact significant enough to move my stuck couple forward. To my frustration, that million-dollar move too often remained just out of reach. Twelve years in practice, and I was once again a beginner, dumbstruck, as I struggled to incorporate a new theoretical model that would take years to master.

Until my workshop with Ellyn, I'd believed that my skill set as a therapist was decent—not fabulous but certainly adequate, and definitely no worse than most of my colleagues'. And though I'd found my couples sessions to be the most challenging hours in my week, though I often left the office exhausted, I had never once considered that part of the problem might be me.

Week in and week out, I'd do what I and most other therapists had been taught, which was to help my distressed couples patch things up as best they could: to be a little bit nicer, feel a little bit closer, take the necessary steps toward meeting each other halfway. And except for couples like Bruce and Cindy, most left my office feeling better than before they'd come in— though, to my chagrin, their progress often unraveled within a matter of days. Mostly I thought the problem was them, that they were too difficult, too argumentative, too stuck in their ways. Sometimes I thought that marriage was the problem, that it's really too hard for most of us to have a marriage that works.

Then I learned that all this struggle makes sense. I'd been given a new lens through which to view people's marital difficulties: symbiosis; low levels of differentiation; developmental stasis. Those terms alone explained ninety percent of the strife that my couples experienced. No wonder they all seemed tied up, as if bound together in some emotional three-legged race, lacking the ability to step apart when necessary and unable to tolerate the tension of their separateness when they did.

As I continued my studies, I realized the wisdom of the old adage "The more you know, the more you realize how little you know." I found myself having more questions than answers. As soon as one bit of new theory began to make sense, it was quickly replaced by another that left me baffled once again. Had I misjudged the friendly closeness in one of my couples? They looked warm and cooperative on the surface, but were they more likely conflict-avoidant, desperately keeping the peace at all costs? And the self-sufficiency and independence in my seemingly autonomous newlyweds—were they simply maintaining a comfortable distance due to their poor self-definition and the fears they both had about getting too close?

Maybe, I thought, but how could I be sure?

At the time, I saw only six or seven couples a week in my full-time schedule. Eventually couples would fill most of my days. But in the beginning, I had only one or two chances a day to roll out my brand-new skills and try my hand at inching my clients upward developmentally. To better assess them, I began listening closely to their language, watching their facial expressions and their breath, honing my observational skills in the hope that eventually I would actually know what to do with the things that I saw. In time I began to perceive some consistent patterns.

TROUBLE SIGN 1: COUPLES WHO CAN'T SPEAK WITHOUT UNCONDITIONAL APPROVAL

One of the first things I noticed was how every one of my clients monitored their partner's response to nearly each word that they uttered. "What?" they'd quickly demand, seizing on the barely perceptible lift of an eyebrow, the impatient sound of an exhalation, vigilant to every nuance of reaction for evidence of some perceived judgment, some indication of how the two of them were not perfectly aligned in mirror-image agreement. I was able to spot the subtle ways people pulled at each other for assurance, agreement, and unconditional approval and how they fought or withdrew when it didn't come. When their sameness was threatened, most of my clients freaked out in some way, becoming unable to finish the sentence they'd started, escalating to conflict, shutting down if their partner wasn't, literally or figuratively, holding their hand, immediately saying, "Yes, I hear you; you're absolutely right, and I agree completely."

I watched people whine and blame and capitulate over things about which they felt strongly. Lacking the courage to voice what they wanted, reveal what they believed, hesitant to say "I think we're overspending" or "I'm worried about your drinking," they waffled and then blamed their partner for their own shaky stance.

And every day I saw myself in them.

"I'd really like to save money for retirement, but Philip insists on taking extravagant vacations."

"I'm not allowed to talk about sex. If I even try, Lisa freaks out."

"I have no voice in this marriage," I heard countless spouses lament, contending that everything had to happen on their partner's terms.

So he insists? So she freaks out? It's amazing how when faced with our partner's pushback, so many of us will fail to take a stand for what we truly believe, even when the stakes are extremely high. What I'd learned was true: it *is* deadly to compromise your core values. When we do, we damage ourselves and the vitality of our relationship. Yet in the lives of most couples, this goes on all the time—with consequences more dire than they imagine.

One man I worked with remained silent for years about his wife drinking two or three martinis after work and then driving to pick up the twins from Hebrew school. Again and again, she'd insisted she was perfectly sober, so rather than have a big fight every Tuesday and Thursday, he instead shut his eyes and prayed that the next time he saw his loved ones would not be at the morgue. To this day he feels sick thinking about how, for the sake of keeping the peace, he'd knowingly put his children in harm's way.

Then there was the couple who repeatedly deferred talking about when to have children. The wife figured her husband would eventually come around, so she bowed to his insistence that he wasn't quite ready, that he needed a little more time, and besides, she couldn't possibly want him to say yes solely because he'd felt pressured. Eleven years later, she was forty-three years old and sadly discovered that she'd waited too long.

Why do we hesitate to reveal our true values, to stand by what we believe? Why are we reluctant to speak the "unspeakable"? Why not keep the issues we know must be addressed front and center? *What are we all so afraid of?* I wondered.

Like unwitting laboratory mice, my clients were subject to my trial-and-error experiments, with my results being sometimes effective, occasionally brilliant, always unpredictable, and rarely replicable.

Like the time I'd done everything I could think of to rein in a particularly combative couple's nasty name-calling fight— including my tried-and-true line: you guys are wasting your money, paying to do here what you can do at home for free. At my wits' end, without a moment of forethought, I stood up and said, "I'm going to go outside and water my porch plants. Just give a shout when you're done." The two of them stopped in midsentence and said that maybe, instead, they'd get down to work.

Or the evening I mustered my courage to tell a couple I'd been seeing for nearly a year, "We seem to be going around in circles here, and my hunch is that there's something important that isn't being talked about." Both partners stared at me blankly. The man shrugged his shoulders, while his wife picked lint off her coat sleeve and glanced at the floor. Three days later, she called to say she'd been having an affair and wanted my help bringing it up in our next session, adding that along with feeling terrified, she was also relieved.

A few weeks later, I made the very same move with a couple who also seemed to be spinning their wheels. After the blank stares and the repeated "I have no idea," instead of prompting some great revelation, my words ended up having no impact whatsoever, the three of us silent as I scrambled to come up with what to say next. *What now?* I wondered, still convinced I was right about there being some undisclosed lie. (As I found out later, I was.)

TROUBLE SIGN 2: COUPLES WHOSE ACTIONS DON'T MATCH THEIR WORDS

Practice led to increased understanding, which led to my next set of questions as I struggled to make sense of the troubling behaviors I observed in my clients—behaviors that had, until then, escaped my attention. One of the most striking was how people's actions often contradicted their words. Like the clients who told me that they longed to feel closer while every night they both went to bed with their nose in their laptop. Or the husband who said he'd forgiven his wife's extramarital affair, yet for years, when they'd fought, he had trotted it out as evidence that her decisions were flawed. *Are they deceiving themselves*, I wondered, *or are they just unaware? How's that different from lying, all of them saying one thing and then doing another?*

One woman told her partner, "I want to know what you think," and then flipped out when she went ahead and spoke up. Another said she wanted her husband to take more responsibility with the kids, yet she stepped in the moment he wasn't doing things her way. And every day I heard people say that they wanted change in their marriage and saw them do nothing at all to create it. Not one of them recognized the contradiction between their statement and their actions until I pointed it out.

We all have ways of justifying our behaviors, some of them so habitual that we don't pause to question them. In order to grow, client and therapist alike must have the ability to see themselves clearly, which includes looking at and owning up to their self-deceptions and recognizing the dilemmas they're hoping to sidestep. No one likes being confronted with the ways in which they're inconsistent. Nor is any of us comfortable seeing how we're being cowardly or betraying our values. Even when faced with pushback, it was my job to keep people focused on the difficult issues. My work was—and is—to help my clients set a high standard for themselves and then give them the tools they need to reach it.

I spent most evenings reading and reviewing my case notes, listening to tapes of my sessions with clients, catching the subtle ways they avoided self-confrontation, looking forward to the day that the balance would tip, when I would at last have more answers than questions.

HEAL THYSELF

Though professionally I was wobbling on training wheels, still straining to reach the pedals, at home it was more like riding a roller coaster with no safety harness. I'd been given clear instructions about how to confront my clients' self-defeating behaviors and hold them accountable for the goals they'd set, but in my off-hours, having no couples therapist in residence and no road map to guide us, I was making everything up on the fly. At times I was thrilled at the prospect of shaking things up, questioning our long-held beliefs and our flawed interactional patterns, hoping to make room for something new and improved.

"Do you think you can ask me for something without raising your voice?" I would inquire. "What about saying what you want instead of making me guess? What do you say we try doing things differently?" I would ask, aiming to de-escalate our conflicts and pressing Patrick to do the same. "Maybe we don't have to keep acting as if we're each other's enemy," I suggested. "How about if the two of us try to calm down?"

Though some of my moves helped, others fell flat. And sometimes my attempts at change made things worse than before, leaving the whole marriage-remodeling idea seeming reckless, bound to shake me up and possibly catapult me right out of my marriage.

Much like my naive expectation that marriage would be more of a delightful adventure than a perilous one, I thought Patrick would embrace this whole business of growing our marriage up. Wasn't he as worn out as I? Wouldn't he breathe a sigh of relief when he saw that I'd come home from the workshop heralding news of great changes to come?

Not exactly. Patrick had not taken to Pete and Ellyn's model with quite the relish that I had, and his response was initially lukewarm at best. Something akin to that old complaint "I didn't ask to be born."

And who could blame him? He hadn't asked for any of this. The questions. The diagnosis of our developmental stasis. The urgency of learning to stand on our own feet. Frankly, neither had I. When I'd signed up for "Surviving and Thriving," I'd been thinking I'd learn to thrive as a couples therapist and survive other people's complicated relationships, having never expected to be confronting my own. In spite of the fact that his marriage was sliding off its foundation, Patrick wasn't interested in the total remodel I had in mind. Our marriage had been serviceable enough, ramshackle and teetering though it was, and as far as he was concerned, I should leave well enough alone.

Try as I might to sell him on my ideas, he took issue with

most things I said, had no interest in reading any of the hand-outs, and had even less interest in following my lead up the developmental ladder. Every bit of it sounded crazy to him: the notion that people need to be able to stand apart in order to be close, the idea that we fought because we couldn't tolerate being separate, the probability that closeness also carried some sort of threat. It seemed to him that I'd gone off the deep end.

I tried many times to explain that we were stuck in Stage Two, fighting in circles because of our lack of resilience, lacking the capacity to be curious and open about each other's concerns. "But there's hope!" I said. "Couples don't have to stay stuck forever. See," I continued, pulling out a worksheet for an exercise that Ellyn had taught us, in which couples practice talking and listening in a way that requires them to risk revealing themselves as well as manage their reactivity—in Pete's words, to be curious rather than furious. "Look," I said, handing Patrick two sheets of paper, one with instructions for the speaker and the other for the listener, roles designated as the "Initiator" and "Inquirer." "The process is called 'I to I,'" I explained, pointing out the clever play on the words *Initiator* and *Inquirer* and the not-so-subtle implication that the exercise was designed to get people more solidly situated in their separate *I*s.

"Ha, ha, get it?" I nudged Patrick gently in the ribs with my elbow. "I to I?" Which elicited a friendly nudge back and an eye roll as well. "It's pretty simple," I went on, ignoring the eye roll. "The initiator raises a subject to discuss, like 'I'm worried about how fast you drive with the kids in the car.' This is the issue one of my couples talked about yesterday, that the guy drives his kids to school in the Porsche and the wife—"

"Is she right," Patrick asked, "that he's driving too fast?"

"Maybe, probably. I have no way of knowing, but that's not the point," I replied.

"What's the point, then?" he asked, impatience showing in the way he emphasized the word *point*. "He either drives too fast or he doesn't."

"The point," I said, a little too sharply, "is for a couple to learn how to talk about difficult issues without getting agitated. Without blaming. The *point* . . . is to remain calm . . ." I took a deep breath and exhaled. Still feeling anything but calm, I said, ". . . rather than flipping out or ending up getting defensive, or bailing. Like . . . most of us do when we start to get anxious." *Good catch*, I thought, having said "most of us" when I really wanted to say "you."

Maybe we should talk about this some other time, I thought, worried that we were fast approaching the edge of our slippery slope.

"Why bother with all this rigmarole?" Patrick eventually asked, tossing the papers onto the coffee table. "Why don't people just sit down and talk?"

Why indeed? I wondered.

"I was just hoping we could try something new," I said, my energy already sunk. "You know, asking questions, being curious instead of devolving . . ."

With that Patrick shrugged and got up to make tea. "Maybe," he said, without turning around.

Better a *maybe*, I thought, than an absolute *no*.

Another day I tried a more personal tack, revealing how in the workshop we'd been asked to look at our first disillusionment and how sad I'd felt, wishing we'd been able to handle our differences better from the start. How much easier it would have been if we'd learned those things earlier on. But that strategy didn't go any better than the others I'd tried. Instead of softening his stance, Patrick accused me of, *once again*, dredging up the past, never being able to let sleeping dogs lie. To him, this whole marriage improvement project was yet another demand I was making, and he wanted no part of it.

Still I kept trotting out my good ideas—papers, articles, paragraphs to read, books to discuss—turning our traditional Sunday morning with tea and the newspaper into a weekly miniseminar, with me at the lectern. I was, of course, failing to consider that Patrick was neither my client nor my home improvement project and fully ignoring the fact that Ellyn's clear directive had been to focus on *myself*.

Fortunately, the other six days of the week I was content to practice my fledgling self-management skills—taking deep breaths instead of firing back some defensive retort, trying to hold on to my point of view despite pressure to conform or recant—hoping that my actions might drag our relationship out of the primordial ooze. But I'd barely get a toe onto dry land before being flattened by Patrick's ever-mounting resistance.

"I don't have time for this nonsense!" he'd rant. Or he'd go off on a riff about how I'd gone to a therapy workshop and had come home totally brainwashed.

"You think I have to listen to this? I don't have to listen to this!" he'd eventually shout before turning on his heel and leaving the room.

Some days he'd call me a differentiation zealot or a Bader fanatic; other days he'd attack the theory and leave me out of it.

"What's so great about separateness?" he'd ask. "Why be married if everyone's just doing their own thing?"

No amount of quoting Pete or Ellyn, Einstein, or, for that matter, Nietzsche ("That which does not kill us . . .") made even a nick of difference.

Yes, I admit, my approach was horrendous. I was as rabid as a convert, the door-to-door salesman trying to persuade a reluctant housewife to buy a new vacuum cleaner. "But my old one works just fine," she'd say over and over, her words falling on deaf ears.

The truth of the matter was that we were no different from almost every couple who sets foot in my office, each of the partners secretly expecting that I'll get the other to change. Most have tried everything they can think of to get the other person to shape up—endlessly, repetitively, and in ways they wouldn't dare to admit publicly. They've poked, prodded, shamed, and threatened. They've blackmailed, cried, yelled, stomped around, and occasionally thrown things. They've frozen their partners out, and they've stormed out of the room—all to little or no avail. Then eventually, having exhausted themselves trying, they have, at last, come to a professional to get the job done right.

Years ago, when Patrick and I went to see our first couples therapist, I had high hopes for what would happen when someone other than me put some effort into changing him. Like most couples I see, when the hour finally arrived, we marched into the therapist's office, each with our version of what had gone "wrong." And though neither of us would have said it outright, we'd both assumed that upon hearing our complaints, the therapist would undoubtedly side with *us*; that she'd recognize who was at fault and needed fixing and promptly turn to our partner and get down to work.

My marriage-remodeling project was, unfortunately, no different from that. After a full year of trying—talking about our developmental stasis, saying how poorly differentiated we were, how we were still immature, pointing out the ways Patrick refused to listen, or how he was incorrigibly hotheaded— I started to wonder if it was time to throw in the towel. I'd begun to feel as if I were dragging all 172 pounds of Patrick's refusal up the steep trail to Half Dome because I was sure both of us would love the view. In fact, I was convinced that the view would be spectacular. And once we got ourselves up to the top, we'd finally be blissfully happy, healthy, and free. If only he would come along. But, figuratively speaking, he was unwilling to hike. And he couldn't give a flying fuck about the view.

Eventually, after doing everything I could think of to get him to surrender and come along peacefully, I began to think, *Maybe I'm going about this in the wrong way.* Perhaps I was missing some key piece that might make a difference. I'd heard Ellyn say "Challenge yourself. Take a risk." But what did that really mean? As far as I was concerned, I *was* challenging myself.

Let's say I could never sell Patrick on a new and improved marriage. Let's say he stuck to his guns that things were fine as they were, that I was reaching for some pie-in-the-sky marriage that could never be had. What then? Had my worst fear come true, that we'd traveled too long and far down the wrong road and there was no turning back?

Fortunately, just before thinking *Yes, it's time to give up*, I caught sight of what I was doing. All that sweat and exertion, and there I was, having barely passed Go, still waiting for Patrick's nod of approval, still in need of consent and consensus, expecting that we'd do our growing in lockstep. I'd been paying so much attention to our *we* that I'd been ignoring the work I had to do on my *I*. It was symbiosis all over again.

I'd married a man who was wary of change and threatened by demands. Had I really thought that when faced with my insistent ideas for a complete overhaul of our marriage, he'd say, "Good idea. Sign me up"? Idiotic as that seems, that's precisely what I'd thought. I'd been expecting some mild resistance, but I'd assumed that once he saw how much better things could be, he'd agree. We'd at last be a team, transforming our marriage *together*.

It was then that I knew this work was going to be more arduous and far lonelier than I'd first imagined. Not impossible but different from my original expectation. If my marriage was going to change, I was going to have to change it myself.

IT TAKES ONLY ONE

From the very first afternoon in that first weekend with Ellyn, I was aware that changing my marriage would begin with changing myself. What I didn't fully grasp at the time was that changing myself would be most, if not all, of the work.

For years I'd been longing for change in my marriage, but I'd believed it takes two to create it. I thought marital change was predicated on having mutual goals and a shared vision of how to attain them. Without Patrick's buy-in, what was the point? What was the point of one person giving it her all while the other watched from the sidelines or, worse, got in her way? The point, I discovered, is that unilateral action *is* what creates change in a marriage. Almost all change comes about when one person has an idea and then goes about realizing it. Most of us have been so steeped in the notion that it takes two to create change that we find it hard to believe that radical change can be brought on by one steady and determined partner working to move things in a positive direction.

Sure, we all hope our partners will be open to change—especially when those changes are the ones *we* envision. And yes, at our best, most of us aspire to be collaborative builders of the marriage we inhabit, to have a shared commitment to growth, to go into the process with both feet. But change in a couple doesn't arise spontaneously, and rarely does the inspiration for change strike both partners simultaneously. More often, it's a matter of one partner who has a vision for change and is willing to go out on a limb to attempt to make that change happen. One partner who is willing to risk, to raise his or her standards, refusing to cave in. One partner who tolerates the anxiety of entering new territory. When one partner changes how he or she operates in the marital system, it will inevitably change the system as a whole.

Still, the idea that positive change in a marriage can arise from unilateral effort is foreign to many of us and is frequently perceived to be flat-out wrong. Sure, people concede the idea that both partners in a couple have to work on themselves, but the idea of one person acting as the lone agent for change flies in the face of beliefs that few couples would think to challenge, such as the notion that marriage is a two-way street, that each person will do his or her share, pull his or her own weight, that life will be fair, that we'll meet each other halfway; that things in a marriage will be shared fifty-fifty.

Fifty-fifty? *Really?* What about when it's forty-sixty or ninety-ten? What about the countless times when one person unilaterally longs for something new to occur? What happens when one person wants to move out of the city or have a third child, to take longer vacations or save more for retirement, to have sex in the kitchen or in broad daylight—and not just on Sunday? And what happens in the event that you enthusiastically put forth your fifty percent and your partner does zip?

When I first suggest to my clients that change in a marriage requires that one or both partners make unilateral moves, many are skeptical—and some are incensed. "Why should *I* be the one to do all the work?" they protest, as if unilateral change, by definition, means they'll be carrying their partner's deadweight. For some, the word *unilateral* carries a negative connotation, as if it implies permission to be inconsiderate or self-serving. "What are you saying, it's every man for himself?" one client demanded, thinking that I was condoning making moves at the expense of one's partner, trying to get what we want by whatever means necessary—an assumption that couldn't be further from the truth.

Others protest the idea that they should have to go first. "Why waste my effort?" they ask. "Obviously he's got no interest in growing." Or "If she wanted this change, she'd have initiated it herself." "And besides," they add, "it doesn't mean as much to me if I have to ask." It isn't hard to imagine what can happen to a couple when both partners have this belief, waiting a lifetime for the other to lead the way to a more satisfying life.

Along similar lines, many people claim that they're tired of "always" being the one to bring things up, hoping their spouse will eventually share that sometimes burdensome job. As with the exasperated wife in one of my favorite cartoons: finally worn out by her husband's resistance, she says, "O.K., we'll try it your way—let's ignore any problems that come up in the next twenty years and see what happens." This is good for a chuckle, but those of us in her position (in heterosexual relationships it's most often the female, though I've seen some exceptions) wouldn't tolerate this arrangement for a week, or a month, let alone twenty years. In most relationships there's one person who acts as the guardian of the relationship, tending as one might tend to a garden, seeing that it's well watered, well fed, and properly weeded. Like it or not, it's a job taken on by the partner most suited—a crucial role that, once defined in this way, can be not only accepted but embraced for the gift that it is.

Then there are those with the mistaken idea that changing oneself to improve one's marriage is a veiled suggestion that, for the greater good, we must change into the person our partner wants us to be. Were I to become more punctual or more tolerant of mess, or were Patrick to come in the door and hang up his jacket (along with his backpack, and hey, while we're at it, how about those shoes and the collection of pocket change on the dining room table?), there's no question that some tensions would ease. But the changes that would benefit us the most had to do with how we handled our differences, not how we eliminated them. For me to be happy in my marriage, I needed to become steadier on my feet when Patrick criticized me or disputed my point of view, rather than crumbling or lashing out in frustration. And I needed to be more open-minded about his wants and concerns—a behavior change far more important than learning to get out the door lickety-split. Often, the real changes one partner needs to make don't even show up on their partner's top ten list, and in some cases, those changes are outright unwelcome—as with a couple in which one partner needs to develop enough backbone to confront an issue such as drug use or gambling that, due to the couple's collusion, has long been ignored.

Be it unilateral or otherwise, few of us embrace change as readily as we claim to. In fact, most people I know have considerable resistance to change. "Why mess with a good thing?" they ask. "Why not leave well enough alone?" Much like Patrick when I presented him with the blueprint for our marriage remodel, people often insist that things are fine as they are.

"Better the devil you know than the devil you don't," one client liked to say, though he'd be the first to admit that the devil he knew was making him miserable.

But this nearly universal reluctance to change isn't because we're a nation of cowards. Stepping into the unknown is risky, and our brains are designed to be adverse to risk. "Change is dangerous," says your brain. "Why take a chance?" Never mind that the conditions of your life are unbearable. Your brain's primary concern is to keep you alive.

It's no surprise, then, that when we consider change, our anxieties rise. *What's going to happen?* we wonder, as we start to have second thoughts. *Will I be defenseless in the face of some unforeseen consequence? Am I strong enough to handle this, come what may? And what if I'm not?*

When Ellyn said to go against our instinct for self-preservation, she had in mind that when push comes to shove, that instinct will tell us to simply stay put. Just as it did as I drove home from that first weekend workshop: *It's a suicide mission*, it said. *Don't dare to risk.*

But let's say that despite all the reasons to protect ourselves, we muster the courage to forge ahead anyway. Let's say that we give up the fantasy about things needing to be fifty-fifty and accept the novel idea of unilateral change. If we stop worrying that we'll be the only person making any changes at all and trust that our positive efforts may inspire the same in our partner (though we have no guarantee), the question to consider is *Where do I begin?*

Having exhausted all other options and finally embracing

the idea that all change in a marriage begins with one person, I took yet another step into unexplored territory, prepared to have that person be me.

The Takeaway:
Don't Be Afraid to Change First

- You can't cajole or wheedle your way into a better marriage.

- Most of us want our partner to change so that we don't have to change ourselves.

- If you want to have a better marriage, be willing to take the first step. It's courageous to be the front-runner for change.

– Part Two –

NOW WHAT DO I DO?

How to Implement Change by Yourself

4

IT GETS A LOT EASIER
ONCE YOU KNOW WHAT TO FIX

If what you're doing isn't working, try something new

All things being equal,
the simplest solution tends to be the best one.
—WILLIAM OF OCKHAM

Focusing on myself brought an immediate payoff. Our first squabble, which was about my favorite sweater ending up in the dryer, provided a key piece of information about my part in our mess. Thirty seconds in, I realized that the only reason we were having a fight was that when Patrick got defensive, I followed suit in an instant.

Several days later a minor clash about whether or not I was grumpy made it clear that no topic was too absurd for me to debate. Several other fights revealed that I too quickly interpreted a groan or an eye roll as a declaration of war. There was also plenty of evidence that I was just as likely as Patrick to send off the first volley—and equally likely to insist on my innocence.

Up until then, I'd been an expert about Patrick's wrongdoings and a novice about mine. Sure, I'd given lip service to the notion that we all play our part, that it takes two to tango, but until I made the commitment to pay attention to my part alone, my role in our troubles remained poorly defined. How could I possibly expect to change my marriage unilaterally if I had no clear idea of what I needed to change?

One particularly difficult day, when I was sure my whole marriage-saving effort was worse than banging my head against a brick wall, I heard myself whisper, "Try something new." Patrick and I had been going around and around in our usual manner about whether or not I was a nag for, yet again, asking everyone to clear their books-shoes-soccer balls-backpacks-jackets-newspapers-notebooks-staplers-spoons-teacups-computer bags-cereal bowls-house keys-homework-junk mail-glue sticks-string cheese wrappers-and-calculators from the kitchen table so we could set it for dinner. I'd been able to keep my cool in the argument for a mere handful of seconds before Patrick's critical retorts set me ablaze.

"If people did what I'd asked the first time, I would only have to ask once!" I shouted.

"You *never* ask once!" Patrick shot back.

"That's because nobody picks up their stuff!"

"That's because you're a nag!"

"No. Nagging is what happens after people don't do what they're *asked*."

"No. Nagging happens when people ask over and over."

"Nobody needs to ask *over and over* when people pick up their *crap*!"

"Maybe people would pick up their *crap* if you would stop *nagging*!"

Three times around the block on this, and I was on the verge of a meltdown. *Slow down*, said a calm, quiet voice in my head. *What's going on?* My first impulse was to say "Patrick's being a jerk" and just leave it at that. But given my commitment to learn from our fights, it seemed like a good idea to look further. What was going on was that we were, for the ten millionth time, caught in a cycle of blaming and deflecting blame, with no way to exit. What was also going on, I realized, was the tendency I'd been slowly becoming aware of: that when wrongly accused, I would fight to the death.

This could go on all evening, I thought, dreading the prospect. Unless, of course, one of us found a way to let go.

Earlier that day, a couple in my office had been having a nearly identical fight, using the word *tyrant* instead of *nag*. In midsentence the husband paused, shaking his head, as if to acknowledge that he should have known better. "Never argue with an idiot in public," he said, quoting Plato. "When people come by, they'd have no way of telling which one of you is the idiot."

No kidding, I thought, also shaking my head. All those hours wasted making much ado about nothing; conflicts sparked by little more than a shrug or a simple request. As if it actually mattered who washed the sponge. There were days that Patrick and I might easily have found ourselves arguing about whether the earth was round, if one of us were to vehemently insist it was flat.

Though I was still riled up about being called a nag, I decided just to let the fight drop. Patrick had the last word—something about support groups for the compulsively neat—while I remained silent, literally biting my tongue; determined, for once, not to be mistaken for an idiot.

THE SURPRISING WAYS
WE SABOTAGE OUR OWN GROWTH

Right around the time when I was embarking on my quest to remodel my marriage, a client gave me a small book of motivational quotes. Along with the old standards—"A journey of a thousand miles begins with a first step" and "The only thing to fear is fear itself"—there were a few gems that, to my surprise, actually helped inspire me. One was "If you do not change direction, you may end up where you are heading." Another was "A quarrel is quickly settled when deserted by one party. There is no battle unless there be two." Best of all was a quote from Winston Churchill, who wisely advised, "When you're going through hell, keep going." That one is in a frame on the wall of my office.

Most days I marched on with a warrior's spirit, while other days not even Churchill could inspire me to keep going. Like the day after our tedious go-round about nagging, which had for some reason sent me into despair. Although unhooking from our fight was without question a victory, and in many respects I should have been pleased about it, when I looked to the future and how far we still had to go, all I could think was that we'd be at this forever.

Perhaps I was kidding myself, thinking that, in spite of our quarreling, Patrick and I were on the road to repair. What if we'd deviated too far from any sane definition of normal marital strife? But then I remembered the story about Pete and Ellyn cautiously eyeing each other at the rim of the Grand Canyon. Obviously even their marriage had seen its share of rough days. Yet there they eventually were, smiling, at peace, standing together, toes to the edge. The advice columnist Dr. Joyce Brothers had a similar story: "My husband and I have never considered divorce," she said. "Murder sometimes, but never divorce."

I thought about the couples in my practice and the few of our friends who had managed to stay married in the age of divorce. Every one of those marriages had seen its peaks and its valleys. Every partner had, at some point, dreamed of escape. I'd been working for years to have a happier marriage, and sometimes I'd have sworn I'd been at it for a lifetime. Clearly I'd underestimated how long and difficult a pursuit it would be. All evidence pointed to the fact that the journey from an entangled, emotionally reactive relationship to a loving partnership where people are solid and steady is slow and fraught with detours and setbacks. Forward movement would better be measured in inches, not miles.

So I turned once again to the wisdom I could glean from my ongoing couples therapy training, reading everything I could find in the library about how people change—what gets in the way and what makes change more likely, what makes some people collapse while others bounce back. Surely there had to be *something* in all this material that could help move things along.

And it turned out there was. The course materials from one of the first Couples Institute workshops I'd taken had a list* of typical thoughts and behaviors that people use to avoid the risk taking and hard work that growth requires—behaviors applicable to conflict avoiders and fighters alike. *Perfect*, I thought, not having realized until then that I'd overlooked its value.

These weren't just some bothersome ways of thinking and acting, as I'd originally assumed. This was a list of behaviors that will bring a person's self-development to a standstill. Behaviors such as whining and complaining, playing the martyr, thinking your partner is what stands between you and bliss. The list was a page long, and I was guilty of at least half of the items on it. Sometimes I'd hidden my feelings, while at other times I'd carelessly blurted them out. I'd also given up when my first attempts at change didn't go well and had overindulged in self-pity, deeply convinced that I had it worse than most others. Continuing on down the list, I owned up to believing that Patrick was the source of our troubles and also assuming that he wasn't capable of change—at which point I was batting a thousand. There were a few bad behaviors that were not in my repertoire, such as plotting ways to get even and putting on a fake smile, as well as trying to pretend that things didn't bother

---

* You can find the complete list in the appendix, page 255.

me at all. I was also not one to numb my feelings with alcohol or drugs, nor was I inclined toward seeing suffering as a virtue.

I was, however, guilty of focusing on all the things that seemed wrong, which only served to turn challenges into catastrophes. Similarly, I'd let myself get so flooded with discouragement that I was unable to see a path forward. Several points talked about getting overbusy or finding distractions, which I'd certainly done. When things were going badly, I'd thrown myself into work or elaborate gardening projects or focused on the kids and just tuned Patrick out. And as many people do, when I felt totally miserable, I'd consoled myself with fantasies of leaving—never once considering any of those behaviors to be the avoidance that they were.

When I first looked at the list, I'd found all of the points to be eye-opening. But the most startling of all was—fighting! It was right there in black and white. One of the key ways to prevent your own growth: "Have a nasty fight."

Instead of *what*? I wondered.

For years I'd believed that our fights were legitimate attempts to work things out—despite our going in circles and both ending up hurt; despite wearing us out and eroding our goodwill. I'd assumed that with all the words we exchanged, we were communicating something important, that we were solving our problems, when in fact we were simply too emotionally flooded and distracted to recognize them. I understood, now, that our real problem was that we were still attempting to obliterate our differences, acting as if our lives depended upon gaining consensus. Resisting the hard work of standing alone.

But the alternative to fighting was hard to picture. I was certain it wouldn't be stuffing things under the rug, nor minimizing difficulties we really needed to confront (two additional points on Pete and Ellyn's list). It seemed too big a leap to imagine that Patrick and I would ever get to a place where we'd have a life with *no* fighting, but I *could* imagine learning to handle myself differently in the fights that we had.

Though any fight would be a great place to practice, I was eager to take on the most challenging of all: the "loopy logic" fights that always left me demoralized. Just picturing myself standing steady and solid within that whirlwind of words convinced me that I'd found the right course of action. Best of all, Patrick would be helping me grow by not changing a thing.

All along I'd been hoping to discover a road map that would lay out my steps, but for the first time I realized that a map was unnecessary. Now I had a clear goal in mind: to function like an adult when we were in conflict, to keep my thinking brain in gear and my emotions in check, to keep from blowing up or melting down or spinning in circles the way I'd done for years.

What would that take? I could not know in advance. All I could do was bring an adventurous spirit, to think of myself as an innovator or an explorer; to be willing to try this and try that, to test my hypotheses about how I might best keep my footing, fully expecting at least some of them to fail.

With this as my mission, I couldn't wait to get started. Not that my intention was to straight away pick a fight. *No need*, I realized. Our next fight was certainly just on the horizon.

FALL SEVEN TIMES, STAND UP EIGHT:
BE PREPARED TO FAIL BEFORE YOU SUCCEED

Winston Churchill once said that courage is being willing to go from failure to failure without losing enthusiasm, a message more empowering than his other standby, "Never give up." Though perseverance is useful, better still is the idea that success is the last stop after a long series of mishaps.

I kept this in mind as I struggled to find a way to reliably steady myself in the midst of a conflict. I discovered, for example, that I felt stronger and more clearheaded when I argued while standing up. But that alone was no guarantee of success. I tried slowing things down by asking questions such as "What do you mean?" or "Could you explain that?" or simply saying "Hold on"—a complete waste of time, since when Patrick was upset it was full speed ahead.

Try as I might, I was still unable to keep my thoughts straight when Patrick was challenging them. Over and over, I'd try my best to remember what I'd wanted to say; to go ahead and say it; and then do my damnedest to remember what I truly believed. I often felt as though I were playing the memory game we'd played with the kids on long car rides: apple, berry, cat, dog, elephant, firefly, adding a new word each time while attempting to keep them all straight in my head. When I was fighting with Patrick, all the words disappeared.

Several months into my experiment, I decided to try a new move. When I found myself getting dizzy, frustrated, or about to melt down, my plan was to take a time-out. I believed that my only hope for success lay in stepping far enough away from the action to maintain my grip—even if that meant leaving the room.

The first time I did it, Patrick was stunned. "You're bailing midstream!" he said, as if the far shore of our fight were a destination worth reaching. We'd been arguing about my being late, one of our perennial favorites. I'd said I'd be ready to take a walk at four thirty. It was four thirty-six before I came downstairs, and even then I was still searching around for my sweatshirt and hat. To me four thirty-six is the same as perfectly on time, but he'd been waiting, he said, having, "in all honesty," preferred three thirty or four. Four thirty was simply the time to which he'd reluctantly agreed. He'd much preferred four, he repeated. In fact, he'd done me a favor, but, *as always*, he said, I had pushed it too far.

"It's not a big deal," I replied, kidding myself that I was being at all helpful. "I'm ready to go," I said cheerfully, which wasn't quite true. I'd be ready once I checked the back door and retied my shoe, and while in the kitchen it seemed like a good idea to drink some water. "Can I get you a cup?" I asked, at which point Patrick blew.

"Four thirty is four thirty, and now it's nearly five!"

"It's actually four forty-nine," I said curtly, and things went downhill from there.

With each sentence he spoke, he got louder and louder, saying the same things again and again: I was rude, inconsiderate, I couldn't tell time—at which point I felt myself getting lightheaded and starting to sweat.

"Wait," I said, raising one finger as if I needed to run off to the bathroom or answer the phone. I took one step back and then another, then realized that the only way to keep my thoughts straight would be to walk out the door. The look on Patrick's face was as if I'd broken some law. Apparently, written into our unspoken rules of engagement was the notion that once begun, no fight is too senseless or futile not to be dragged to its miserable conclusion; by "sticking with it" we were not only fulfilling our commitment to each other but earnestly attempting to work through our difficulties. Calling time out was an act of foul play.

"I'll be right back," I said quietly as I stepped out the front door into the blue light of early evening.

Ahhh. Within seconds I began to feel better, slowing like a speeding car rolling to a stop.

I stood in the cool air as one by one the streetlights flickered and then lit. In the distance a dog was barking, and my neighbor across the street was practicing the violin. Down the block the retired schoolteacher was lugging bag after bag of groceries up the stone walkway to her door. Composure regained, head more firmly fastened on my shoulders, I took a deep breath, ready to reenter the fray, prepared to step out again if I needed to do so.

During my absence, Patrick had not moved an inch. Even once I returned, he remained utterly speechless and uncharacteristically calm, as if the fight, left unattended, had simply burned itself out.

With this success, I now had a plan: every time we fought, I would move myself off of and back onto the field of battle, training myself to become more steady and calm. In hindsight, this was precisely what I needed. Each time I paused to compose myself, I was learning to still my anxiety in the electric presence of Patrick's. Unwieldy and inelegant as it was, slowly but surely, after many months of trying, my do-it-yourself approach paid off.

HOW ONE PERSON CAN
QUIET THE WHOLE ECOSYSTEM

When I first met my clients John and Celeste, it was like looking back in time at Patrick and me. They were young and newly married, headstrong and softhearted, easily hurt and quick as lightning to flare. Once into a conflict, they were as locked in as we'd been: unable to unhook or calm down or maintain any perspective, both awash in anxiety at the first hint of discord.

Ten minutes in a room with them, and I was nearly as dizzy as I'd been when it was Patrick and me in a fracas. I couldn't very well walk out of the room during their therapy session, so being able to remain cool and steady, clear-thinking and anxiety-free in their presence required every bit of solid self that I had acquired. Especially when things between them went wild—which happened approximately once every five minutes.

Unlike Patrick and me, who fought mostly in the car or the kitchen, their fights were multimedia events: conducted face-to-face in my office and in their home, on cell phones, in text messages, through emails and countless hours of instant messaging. They were two cyberwarriors who could print out their reams of contention to relive them, line by line, or review them like notes transcribed by a court reporter. If I had agreed to it, they would have cc'd me on every exchange.

Gosh, I thought, when they first described their IM fights. Could they really keep it up from afar? Just getting some physical distance was usually enough to pull the plug on my fights with Patrick. How could they get anything done, cyberbickering all day? "You do this while at work?" I asked in astonishment. Apparently so.

Sessions with them were a challenge as I did whatever was necessary to psychologically "seat belt" myself into my chair: my feet literally on the floor at all times, my breath slow and even. Thank God I'd done enough work on myself to be developmentally at least ten steps ahead of them. No matter how loud or wild it got, I spoke softly and firmly (a trick I had learned from my son's kindergarten teacher), sometimes repeating their names, as if trying to wake them from a nightmare. They reeled out their mind-numbing content: "You said you would call." "No, I said I would text." "No, you didn't." "Yes, I did." "No, I have it, right here on voice mail." Meanwhile I watched how poorly or well they managed their reactions and gently nudged them in the direction of self-exploration instead of knee-jerk blame, anxiety management instead of reactive self-protection. It took many, many months, but eventually they began to quiet down. In baby-step fashion, they learned to pause before firing back or collapsing into a crumpled heap of defeat, bemoaning the impossibility of getting through to the other. Slowly but surely they ceased needing a referee. Better still, they were willing to consider no longer fighting by text.

Much the way most people change, their progress had been three steps forward and two steps back. So, no surprise, they showed up one session shooting daggers, sitting as far apart from each other as they possibly could while still being in the same room.

They'd gotten into a row about the politics of coffee. He'd come home from the market with a pound of French roast that was obviously not shade-grown. And beyond that it wasn't even organic, the two qualifications she'd explained many times. "What do you want, for me to start my day drinking pesticide?" she'd asked. "It was on sale," he'd said. She'd then shot him a look and stormed out of the kitchen, accusing him of never paying attention to the things she finds important.

"I'm afraid you don't love me anymore," John said. "When we fight, you look at me as if I'm some sort of villain. I see it in your eyes . . . you hate me. And I think, 'Oh . . . it's over. She's leaving me.'"

Celeste stared at him in silence. In all the time I'd been seeing them, rarely had there been a word spoken that hadn't been a complaint, a criticism, or a rebuttal of a previous attack. A statement as vulnerable as this was unprecedented. And never had there been even a moment of silence.

"Why in the world would you think that I hate you?" Celeste finally asked.

"Why would I think that?" John frowned, incredulous. "Because you said it, that's why."

"Oh," Celeste replied.

In the high tide of anxiety, people say all kinds of things. Mean things. Angry things. *I hate you. I'm leaving. I never loved you.* Words fly out of our mouths, relieving the tension of the moment, only to be deeply regretted later. Or we hurt without words with a snort or a groan, looking away in disgust or narrowing our gaze with disdain. At times we intend to hurt, while other times we're so flooded with anxiety that we're simply firing randomly at anything that moves.

In their nonstop war of words, John and Celeste had failed to notice the precision of their aim: that their words hit their target, that what they said *hurt*. They saw themselves, instead, as innocents, each in his or her own little village under siege, hunkered down in their foxholes, when in fact they were both tossing out grenades, mystified that life together felt like a war zone.

"I'm sorry," Celeste said as they were leaving the session, promising to pay attention to her words, to soften her stance, even if John did not change a thing.

At their next session she told me she'd made good on her vow. She'd stopped giving John dirty looks and hurling barbed insults, even though, she admitted, she was frequently tempted. Now and again she'd even said something nice. And in this more temperate climate John responded in kind.

Several weeks later, Celeste reported that things were continuing to improve. She and John were fighting less and having more fun. They'd gone out with friends and had a long weekend away.

"How do you account for the change?" I'd asked them, thinking it was possible that they'd merely misplaced their cell phones.

At first all Celeste could say was "Things feel different." And "I've changed."

And although she was grateful for the increasing tranquillity at home, the changes she had been experiencing within herself were unsettling, disorienting. "Welcome but weird" was how she put it.

"What you've been telling us is sinking in," she said. For months, I'd been asserting that the two of them were like kindling easily sparked by the other's words and that they needed to learn to calm down around each other, not to go up in flames each time the other dropped a match. I'd repeatedly said that it takes only one person quieting down to quiet the whole system; we have choices about what to do and how to respond, no matter what our partner has said or done. She'd been watching me in the sessions, she added. How I take deep breaths when they get riled up, how I pause before speaking.

"Not that it's easy, by any means," she added. "The other day I totally lost it. We were talking about where to go eat. John mentioned some hamburger place, and I said, 'Oh, that's the one my brother said we ought to check out,' and he just blew up. He said I interrupted him, but I thought he was done. Then he said I was rude, but I disagreed. I wasn't rude; I thought he was done. He kept at it, saying I was interrupting, and I ended up screaming at him. And then he got that 'Oh, aren't you a nutcase' look on his face. Finally I just threw the newspaper at him and walked out," she said, shaking her head.

"I hate when he accuses me of things I haven't done," she added, glancing at John and then back to me. "Then I heard your voice in my head: 'If he says you're covered in green polka dots, does that make it true? Do you have to argue with him about it? Does it actually matter?' Thinking that made me laugh. 'You're letting him control you,' I told myself, like I was channeling you," she said, smiling at me. "Then the whole thing evaporated. I was completely calm. I could see it was totally stupid, like I've been completely insane all this time and I suddenly woke up normal.

"See what I mean by weird?" she asked, facing me, her expression a mixture of curiosity and concern.

I knew exactly what she meant. The first time I'd been able to stay in the room and not get snagged when Patrick tossed out one of his hooks, I, too, had felt odd. It was as if I had traveled to the edge of the earth's atmosphere and by some stroke of magic had popped outside the pull of gravity and was floating in space. Buoyant. Free.

When I'd first devised my "pause and step outside" routine, my goal had been simply to figure out how to think straight under pressure. For many months, I'd go out and cool off, then return to the battleground, only to be rendered useless in short order. At first I'd last ten, maybe fifteen seconds at most before I had to step out again, doing so half a dozen times or more. Most often it was like walking in the wrong direction on an escalator: try as I might, in the end, I'd tire of the effort and sink to the bottom, reduced to tears or shaking with rage.

What I failed to notice was that over time my staying power had risen—incrementally, imperceptibly, but increasing nonetheless. One quiet little brick at a time I was building a house sturdy enough to withstand whatever huffing or puffing Patrick might attempt. One day, a year or so after I'd launched my campaign, we were in one of our typical idiotic go-rounds, and to my astonishment, I didn't need to leave. Minutes passed, and as Patrick's rejoinders made less and less logical sense, I quietly stood there, thinking my own thoughts and having my own ideas about what was going on. No longer a lunatic who couldn't think straight, I was a curious bystander, calmly listening and wondering what in the world was getting him so riled up.

All along I'd been thinking of this process as if it were a battle, thinking in war metaphors, reading Churchill and Lao-tzu, Douglas MacArthur, Seneca. And although I was right—I had been doing battle—I eventually realized that the battlefield was not where I'd originally thought and the enemy was not the seemingly formidable opponent I'd married. Slowly, it had begun to dawn on me that the progress I'd made, the battle I'd won, was with myself. I'd been wrestling with my automatic way of reacting, struggling with the intense anxiety of standing alone, working to calm myself even while Patrick was egging me on.

I'd set a goal for myself, one that was only about me, and I owed my success, in part, to the worthy adversary who could get to me like no other. For years he'd been testing me, making it hard, knocking me off course; pushing me to the point where I could no longer live life "as is"; frustrating me to the point of change.

The Takeaway:
It Gets a Lot Easier Once You Know What to Fix

- Fighting can be one of many ways that we sidestep the challenging work of learning to tolerate our differences. Recognizing (and abandoning) your go-to avoidance moves will speed up your growth.

- Changing even one ineffective behavior can disrupt the familiar patterns of conflict between two people, making room for a healthier outcome.

- Pausing is not an act of capitulation or avoidance. It's a wise, unilateral choice that can change your whole relationship system.

5

KEEP YOUR ANXIETY
FROM RUNNING THE SHOW

Strengthen your tolerance for
the things that push your buttons

A man that flies from his fear may find that he has only
taken a short cut to meet it.
—J.R.R. TOLKIEN, *THE CHILDREN OF HÚRIN*

Julia and Mark sat in my office late one winter evening, our chairs pulled in close so that we could hear each other over the sounds of heavy rain pelting the roof above. The room was warm and bright, in stark contrast to the ominous wind rattling the tree branches outside. We were trying to make sense of where things had gone wrong in their marriage, slowly and methodically retracing the steps that had brought them here: Mark deciding to move out, first staying at the Hyatt, then renting an apartment, considering divorce but not absolutely, totally sure.

I think of them as an eleventh-hour couple—a couple who had come to see me close to the breaking point, far gone into struggle, with little emotional time left before their marital clock strikes midnight. For Julia and Mark, it was more like

11:59 p.m., with several affairs lied about for years and now finally out in the open. Mark admitted to still wanting to see the other woman, Anna, although, at least temporarily, he'd broken it off. He said that he missed her, yet he and Julia were there sitting with me, the three of us asking and answering the hard questions that might give their marriage a second chance.

Mark began with all the issues he and Julia had left unspoken: about the years he had been in law school and they had seen each other one day a week, about Julia's eventual decision to be a stay-at-home mom, despite the financial pressures that had caused, how she seemed so uninterested in sex that he could almost hear her counting down the minutes until it would be over and done with. He talked about his late nights at work, how he'd stay late just surfing the Internet or playing *Angry Birds* because life at home was so painfully empty. How hard it was to look Julia in the eye. How neither of them talked about any of it.

Julia said it was true, it *was* awful between them, and nothing she tried made much of a difference: weekend getaways, date nights, cooking Mark's favorite dinner. Things stayed the same—until they got worse. In order to cope, she kept herself perpetually busy, collapsing into bed at night, thoroughly exhausted, and falling asleep instantly. Mark said that for years he'd been dying inside and revealing nothing.

"Dealing with the hard stuff made me scared. I froze. I didn't know what would come of it. Now, with all that's happened, I regret having not talked about it."

I wrote down his exact words and stared at them, stark and

simple on the paper. *Yes*, I thought, *dealing with the hard stuff scares me, too.*

Who isn't scared at the thought of speaking the truth when the truth is guaranteed to bring down a hailstorm of criticism, trigger a five-alarm rage, or be followed by a week of bone-chilling silence? For some of us, the mere thought of our partner's long-suffering sigh makes us think twice. So we say or do nothing, expecting that life in the comfort zone will remain comfortable indefinitely.

Mark's voice was somber and quavering, the conversation careful and measured, as if we were unwrapping delicate glass figurines wrapped in tissue. "We were growing apart, and I made like it wasn't happening," he said. "I told myself it was just a stage we were in. You know, families with young kids. I told myself it was normal, that we'd eventually get through it. Better that than admit I was too terrified to act."

Clients often use words such as *terrifying* and *dangerous* when they talk about change. They look at me wide-eyed when I suggest that they move beyond the bounds of their self-protection—even when I'm suggesting something that was their idea in the first place. What's the worst that can happen if you go ahead and initiate sex while the kids are downstairs watching TV? Why not say that you're worried about how much time the two of you spend on your iPads, how you sit together at dinner and have nothing to say? What keeps you from saying "Let's slow down when we kiss?" "No," they tell me. "I couldn't possibly say that . . . do that . . . reveal that"; never pausing to question their worst-case scenarios; never considering that playing it safe might be as dangerous in the long run as taking a risk.

Mark and Julia conceded that the years of silence, the way they had ignored glaring issues, the nose-to-the-grindstone busyness—even the affairs—had all come from fear, from avoidance.

"Avoidance of what?" I asked.

Julia said her worst fear was that Mark would say she was demanding—a characteristic that she was raised to believe bordered on sin. "Better to be a good little soldier," she said, repeating a favorite phrase of her father's. "Better to ask for nothing at all."

She had adopted this strategy as a child. As the youngest of ten she'd been rewarded for making due with little, praised for the fact that she rarely cried. No one cared much about who she was, or what she wanted—and they cared even less about what she *felt*. What she had learned as a child, she had carried forward: when you're afraid, when you're sad, when something is wrong, you simply keep moving. You do what you must, and you never, ever look up.

Mark hesitated and then told me that fighting with Julia made him feel sick. Literally. As though he might throw up. "I'd do almost anything to avoid it," he said, "including lie." Even as a boy he had feared confrontation, so with Julia it was no different. The possibility that he'd be scoffed at or rejected if he told Julia he was lonely, he felt miserable, or that things had to change, the likelihood that she'd feel hurt or lash out or insist everything was his fault—any and all of these would have seemed unbearable.

"Worse than that, I suppose, is that I'd tell her the truth and she'd tell me to leave."

"And what if she had?" I pressed. "What might you do then?"

Every day I raise questions like these with my clients, asking them to step closer to what scares them rather than step away from it. *What if she threatens to go on a spending spree . . . air your dirty laundry on Facebook . . . never have sex again? So what if he claims he's perfectly happy and the entire problem is you? What's your next move?*

Eventually, the choice becomes obvious: confront what we fear, or continue to live life as is.

I asked Julia what she thought might happen if she dared to look up, to feel what she felt, to speak the truth that was obvious to both of them.

"I would have been totally overwhelmed," she said, her eyes tearing up. "It would have been like entering a foreign country and having no idea where to go."

ANXIETY CAN KEEP YOU
FROM ACTING LIKE AN ADULT

Many couples I see have a similar story. As trouble brewed in their marriage, they felt powerless to change things. Some say they'd had no idea what to do; others say they'd had plenty of ideas but had been too afraid to suggest them. *I'm afraid she'll use it against me. I'm afraid she'll think I'm weird. I'm afraid he'll tell me I'm trying to be someone I'm not.*

Most say it's their partner who's resistant to change, when the real obstacle is one they've never considered.

Sometimes I joke with my clients and tell them, "The trouble is all in your head. Literally." The trouble, I say, is that you have a brain that's designed to maintain the status quo, and it's better at doing its job than you are at countermanding it. Our brains are not inclined to embrace the unknown, to be open to adventure, to be exhilarated by risk, even though some of us actively seek such experiences. When faced with uncertainty and unpredictability, when there are too many variables beyond our control (as there regularly are in our intimate relationships), our survival-obsessed brain reads the situation as a potential emergency and cries "Danger ahead!" whether or not we're truly in danger. "Better safe than sorry," says our hypervigilant brain, acting with speed at the expense of accuracy. Interpersonal conflict and the anxiety that accompanies it are then easily mistaken for a life-and-death threat—and unfortunately we respond as if our brain must be right.

Suddenly we're sweating or trembling, our bodies lit up with energy. Gone is our ability to maintain perspective, to question our reactions, to talk ourselves down. Without pause, we're ready to flee or attack or play dead. Push any of us in our most vulnerable spot, and the next thing you know we're as green as geckos, living from the reptilian "eat or be eaten" part of our brain, all our good sense and ability to reason commandeered by anxiety.

Remember the last time you totally lost it? Maybe you slammed your favorite cup on the counter and it broke into bits. Or you cursed at your computer or your spouse or kicked a dent in the wall. Then again, you may have gone in the other reptilian direction when your anxiety soared: you froze, went invisible, numbed out, or shut down. Still as stone, as if disappearing into the rocks and leaves you were sitting on—equally as frenzied as those of us who explode, only too terrified to move a muscle.

At that point, you'd hit your anxiety threshold, the pressure inside you having mounted at a rate that exceeded your ability to handle it. Each of us can manage "this much and no more" before our brain goes on overload and we can no longer function. Once in this state, we implode, explode, or check out— whichever works best to relieve the tension inside us.

Long before I began learning about couple dynamics and before I'd begun to study the current research about how the brain responds to high stress, I knew from experience how hard it was to stay calm when my instincts were telling me that I was under attack. I saw it in myself and every one of my clients, all of us far too easily set off by something outwardly insignificant, and quick to see our partner as the enemy. What I hadn't known was *why*: why we're so impressionable and volatile and easily threatened; why people can go, in an instant, from sane person to lunatic with little or no ability to put on the brakes.

Then I encountered the work of the UC Berkeley neuropsychologist Rick Hanson,[1] which provided at least a partial explanation. I learned, for example, that the visceral *whoosh* we feel, that head-to-toe sense of emergency, happens because our brain has responded to a conflict over, say, who forgot to buy milk, with the same flood of cortisol and adrenaline that might be needed if we were being hunted down like a wildebeest, about to be killed. It also explained why my step-out-and-cool-off strategy had been so successful. Taking a break when my anxiety ran high was a way of training myself to stay connected to my neocortex—the part of the human brain that formulates strategies, uses words, thinks things through. The part that has the good sense not to get sucked into an argument about measuring laundry soap. The neocortex is what enables us to learn from our experiences and revise our coping strategies, and it can help us maintain perspective when one or both of the emotionally driven, survival-obsessed parts of our brain threaten to turn us into reptiles.

But for all its wisdom and level-headedness the neocortex is sorely lacking in clout. As a relative newcomer in terms of brain evolution, the neocortex is younger and weaker than its reactive (and often overreactive) counterparts that have been running the show for many hundreds of millions of years. When faced with the powerful brain chemistry that is unleashed by anxiety, the neocortex may just as well be nonexistent.

Which means that it's not your fault that keeping your anxiety in check is as hard as it is. Though it's still your job to find ways to remain calm under pressure and take the risks you must in order to grow, know that your brain is unlikely to be an ally in your effort.

Along with the physiological hurdles we face when trying to remain level-headed, there are psychological issues that impact us as well. Our ability (or inability) to stay steady while anxious is heavily influenced by our emotional development, particularly the development of our separate *I*. None of us leaves home with so perfectly developed an identity, so strong and solid a sense of self, that we never find ourselves wavering. Most of us have to work hard to be clear about what we really think, what we feel, and what we know to be true for us.

"Defining a self or becoming one's own person is a task that one ultimately does alone," says the psychologist Harriet Lerner. "No one else can or will do it for you, although others may try and we may invite them to do so. In the end, I define what I think, feel and believe. **We** do not define what I think, feel and believe."[2]

When under pressure from our partners to be or do what they want, maintaining that clarity becomes all the more challenging. It can seem that the problem is that our partner is pressuring us—if she would only back off; if he'd just stop making demands—but the real issue is our poorly developed sense of self. And that problem is one that only we can fix.

As children we all experienced pressure similar to the pressure we get from our partner: pressure to conform, to please, not to disappoint. In one way or another and to varying degrees, we were pressed by our parents and teachers, our families and our peers, to be more how they wanted us to be and less how we actually are. Maybe not totally different, but definitely "improved." You, minus your wandering mind or your interest in dance or your dream of becoming an astronaut. You with the added bonus of being an extrovert.

Whether we're too much of this or not enough of that—too bossy, too shy, not generous to others—we got a clear message that "being ourselves" might not be the best way to go. While some of us caved in to the pressure, aiming to change ourselves

enough to fit in and be loved, others of us rebelled, defying con-
formity, aiming not to be controlled. Either way, we suffered
the injury of being seen negatively by others.

As a result, many of us arrive at the doorstep of adulthood
feeling unsure of ourselves, not yet able to solidly and securely
define our separate self, to embrace who we are. Nonetheless,
as adults we're asked to show up: to say what we want and
what we think even though we ourselves may not know. (And
if we did know, like Julia and Mark we may be hesitant to say
so.) At the same time, we're pressured by others to yield, to
please, to take the stand *they* prefer. No wonder my IQ took a
nosedive when Patrick pressed hard for consensus. No surprise
he felt stymied when I said "No." The more poorly defined and
wobbly we are, the more anxious we become when faced with
our partner's demands. And the more anxious we are, the less
likely we are to remain steady under pressure.

At times it can seem as though we're confronting an impossible choice: to be ourselves, though we risk being criticized or
rejected, or to give ourselves up, to disappear into the *we* because our *I* does not have strong legs to stand on. Remember,
our brain overreacts to uncertainty, be it internal or external.
Without a firm base beneath us, it makes perfect sense that
we feel anxious when pressured. Of course Mark opted to lie
rather than risk confrontation. Of course he and Julia chose
the familiar safety of silence. Until we are secure enough in
ourselves to step out, to withstand some heat, we will be quick
to react and far too easily hurt, focused on our survival when
we need to be focused on our growth.

THE MANY FACES OF ANXIETY

Most people hear the word *anxiety* and think of sweaty palms and racing hearts. They think of the guy on the airplane who had a panic attack or the time they almost passed out before taking their chemistry final. They recall how on the morning of their wedding they felt so wound up and queasy it was as if they'd had fifteen cups of coffee. Few people think of anxiety as the reason they went whiteout ballistic over their wife's insistence that they "hand over the map."

Why would you call my reaction anxiety?

Most clients are surprised to learn that when they're in a tension-filled interaction with their partner, "nearly all of their emotional responses are being shaped by anxiety"[3]—whether or not they recognize that they're anxious. What else could explain two ostensibly sane people getting into a name-calling uproar over the pronunciation of *mayonnaise* or whether they should turn left or right at the gas station?

Anxiety influences us at every turn, though it can be difficult to distinguish it from our other emotions,[4] particularly when we have defined the word *anxious* too narrowly. Most people will attribute their anxious behaviors to anything and everything but the anxiety they feel. "I'm not anxious," they insist when they've stormed out of a restaurant or called their partner an ass. They say they're insulted or frustrated, that they feel justifiably angry. *She implied I was a cheapskate! He called me a know-it-all!* They maintain that their reaction is a perfectly logical and rightful response to their partner's behavior rather than evidence of their internal unsteadiness.

Anxiety comes in many disguises—not just the dread-filled, bounding-pulse version the term often implies. A broader and more useful definition is that anxiety is any reaction set off by powerlessness or threat—real or imagined.[5] It is the disequilibrium that comes from living in a no-guarantees world, a world in which, like it or not, we have little or no control over, well, pretty much anything—definitely not our spouse and occasionally not even ourselves.

Anxiety is at the root of most of the craziness that goes on in our relationships. The pouting, the blaming, the circuitous bickering, the harsh words exchanged and the hurt feelings that follow, the obsession with winning and losing, and the desperate need for consensus. Anxiety is responsible for every "always" and "never," every threat, and every ultimatum we issue. It is behind the dreams we squelch and the stands we don't take. It plays a part in every affair and the upheaval it generates. Yet the word *anxiety* rarely comes into play.

I once heard from a colleague that the first time he and his fellow psychologists in training were entering the locked ward at the psychiatric hospital, the chief of psychiatry asked how many of them had ever been on the other side of the door. "The people in there are not nearly as scary as you might imagine," the doctor assured. "They're a lot like us, except that we only act like them when we're at home."

When we are inundated by interpersonal anxiety, when we can neither tolerate emotional intensity nor calm ourselves down, of course we behave badly. Of course we spin our wheels. Without being able to identify and address the anxiety that influences us, none of us will be capable of sustained change. No amount of good advice—avoid being dismissive, steer clear of criticism, find things to appreciate, learn to repair—will impact a system so bound by anxiety that it cannot mobilize its strengths.

Imagine if, from the start, Julia and Mark had been able to manage their anxiety instead of trying to escape it; if they'd paid attention to the signs of trouble in their marriage and had taken steps to address them. What if they'd known that, scary or not, dealing with the hard stuff would end up being the very thing that would save them?

STRENGTHENING OUR "ANXIETY TOLERANCE" IN EVERYDAY LIFE

When I was first trying to grasp the concept of managing my anxiety, I pictured a waiter gracefully balancing a heavy tray stacked high with dinner plates, moving like Fred Astaire across the dining room without breaking into a sweat. Was that really possible, to carry one's anxiety instead of getting overwhelmed and then letting it crash in a heap? Having come from a family of anxiety off-loaders (and being one myself), it was hard to envision not exploding or melting down when the pressure was mounting; being able to maintain some measure of sanity instead of coming unglued.

For many of us, the idea that we might increase our "carrying capacity" and learn to tolerate anxiety seems like a suggestion that we hold hands with a mountain lion or learn to walk on hot coals. Why not do all that we can to escape it?

Most of my clients are shocked when I tell them that anxiety is an experience they cannot escape. Trying to avoid it is as futile as trying to avoid gravity. If we have any hope of having a healthy and satisfying relationship, we must learn to function well *despite* feeling anxious. As the Buddhist teacher Pema Chödrön advises, "Get used to the feeling of falling." Rather than panicking and then grabbing whatever automatic behavior we resort to under stress, we must do whatever it takes to keep our wits about us, even though we're working against powerful internal forces that only make the task harder.

Some clients have argued that this is too much to ask. They've thought I was advising them not to feel or express their feelings or that I was saying it's not okay to be mad or to cry. One woman claimed that managing her anxiety would inflame her colitis. Another feared she would start grinding her teeth. Others have argued that I'm proposing the impossible. Like one client who insisted that rage is a Croft family trait and he has the gene. Or another who believed that in order to tolerate his anxiety he would have to turn himself into the Dalai Lama, to which I suggested that taking one or two steps in that direction would be a good start.

Like most skills we acquire, anxiety tolerance increases with practice. But no amount of work on ourselves will grant us so much self-control that nothing will rattle us. With life's inevitable stresses, with the never-ending challenges that marriage presents, anxiety will arise, and our ongoing work is to develop ways to handle it. As we become better anxiety managers, we can better resist the temptation to blow our anxiety out or stuff it down. Anxiety management is the middle path where we hold ourselves together in the face of mounting anxiety, be it our partner's or our own. It's the path along which we go against our instinct to fight, flee, or numb out and instead stay put, letting ourselves feel terrified, outraged, or dizzyingly confused and trusting that in time we will come to withstand the intensity. Like a graceful waiter balancing his tray, we grow increasingly steady through repeated, deliberate practice, failing and succeeding, then eventually gaining mastery: carrying our anxiety instead of running away from it.

Once we are no longer bound by the need to escape our discomfort, we can make more informed choices and take more thoughtful actions, fewer of which we'll regret later. From this more solid place, we are able to take unilateral steps that we know are "right"—even though they're unfamiliar and potentially risky.

Like the step one client took when, despite trembling hands, she firmly insisted that her partner hand over the car keys when he'd had too much to drink. Another refused to concede when his wife claimed that his lateness was the reason she'd gotten a speeding ticket and it was therefore his job to pay for it. Clients have confronted long-standing lies and admitted their own misdeeds; they've made bold moves in bed and surprised themselves when they've gracefully handled their partner's lukewarm reaction.

Don't be surprised if, in the thick of things, you are not lavished with praise for your hard work. In fact, it's more likely that your spouse will try by any means possible to suck you back into the fray. "Look at you taking your deep breaths," one man jabbed. "Aren't you terrific, throwing the first punch and then going all saintly." Meanwhile his wife dug her fingernails into the palms of her hands, doggedly determined not to jab back. One client went as far as to say she wouldn't want to stay married if her husband went through with his plan to stop drinking. These demands to "change back" are what Harriet Lerner calls "countermoves,"[6] prompted by your partner's anxiety about separation and change. It helps to keep the long view in mind: though your partner may or may not admit it, once the dust settles, he or she is likely to be grateful (and perhaps even impressed) that you had the where-withal to raise your own standards and not take the bait.[7]

Learning to manage anxiety is a matter of "try this and try that." What works for one person may be totally useless for another (and what works for us one day may be insufficient the next). Though most people need only one or two go-to strategies, whatever "tricks" we devise, the guiding principle is this: no matter what's happening—no matter how off-the-wall ridiculous one or both of you are—it's your job to unilaterally take control of yourself.

For many people, anxiety management begins with self-talk. Most choose a word or phrase that they repeat to themselves to either keep from getting whipped up or to wind themselves down. One woman stayed in control by reminding herself "This is not about me" when her wife declared her both selfish and untrustworthy for parking the kids in front of a video before falling into bed with a migraine. "A rule is a rule," she'd said, citing their "no screens on schooldays" agreement. Another said that for five minutes straight she internally repeated "Don't say anything" as her husband tore through the house in search of his wallet. In times past she'd have launched into a tirade about his disorganization, which would have undoubtedly ended with shouting and mudslinging. Another client found that he's able to keep from ramping up by closing his eyes and spelling out the word *chill*. I've heard clients say things such as "Let's back up, let's try to listen" and "This isn't going well, let's start again," aiming to keep things from deteriorating in the first place. Many have used the same move to encourage their own risk taking, telling themselves *I know you can do it, this is important*, attempting to calm their fears as they raised difficult issues or tried something new.

Another approach to increasing your anxiety tolerance is to work with the way you experience anxiety in your body. Maybe you stop breathing or your knees lock or sweat drips down your back. Or you react the way I used to react and get so woozy that your thoughts disintegrate before you finish thinking them. The sooner (and more accurately) we're able to identify that what we're experiencing is anxiety, the more likely it is that we'll be able to pause or step back or talk ourselves down before it's too late. And when our anxiety does take over and we do come unglued, recognizing anxiety for the neurochemical storm that it is will at least help us understand what came over us. Like it or not, we'll have many more opportunities to practice.

Though each of us is responsible for managing our own insides, it's tremendously helpful to recognize how anxiety manifests in our spouse. When you find yourself thinking "What's wrong with her?" the answer is quite likely—well, you can guess. I'd never considered that Patrick's narrow-eyed glower was about him and not me, that it was a sign he'd hit the bounds of his anxiety tolerance and I'd be wise to stay calm. Just as my overturning a basket of laundry that he'd just folded meant I'd lost my grip and the worst thing for both of us would be for him to lose his grip, too.

Most of us march right into our partner's brainstorm and promptly get sucked in. Chances are there were warning signs that we failed to notice or ignored—quite likely because we were anxious ourselves. A friend's usually mild-mannered husband started swearing at his suitcase when the zipper got stuck. Just before getting on him for having not packed sooner, she had the good sense to think, *Ahhh, he's feeling anxious about the long drive ahead*, at which point she decided to say nothing and take a shower instead. Watching your partner go from Homo sapiens to reptile may well prompt you to go the same route, when what's needed is for you to plant your feet firmly and do your best to hang on.

Also essential is to identify and deal with our "hot button" issues, the ones that are guaranteed to set us off when they come up with our partner. Let's say you go off the deep end when your spouse interrupts you, or you feel devastated when you get turned down for sex. And not just a little bit devastated. We're talking crestfallen, deep-in-the-abyss devastation, where you feel loathsome and miserable and more desperate by the minute, convinced that you'll never, ever have sex again.

Stop for a moment and ask yourself this: Why is my reaction so over the top?

It's true that none of us likes being told no. Nor do we like being contradicted or disregarded or addressed as if we were eight years old. Still, our overreactions have much less to do with the actual insult than we might think. Tell one person she's acting just like her mother and she might laugh it off (or agree), while another will consider it an out-and-out act of war. Tell me that I've done something wrong when I'm convinced that I haven't, and, well—despite all the work I've done, I still might get bent out of shape.

The trauma expert Dr. Noel Larson explains it this way: "If it's hysterical, it's historical." Once your reaction goes above four on the emotional Richter scale, you can assume that whatever is going on in the present is being intensified by unresolved issues that you've carried from your past. Until we know what's at the root of our anxiety-laden response—what's made it a supercharged issue for us in the first place—we'll end up taking our partner on when it would be far wiser to take ourselves on instead.

When flooded with anxiety, we can easily forget that, difficult as it is, change might actually improve things. Change is sure to make waves, and we cannot know at the outset if we'll be temporarily seasick or cast overboard.

When I was in the midst of my washed-out-to-sea-in-a-riptide experience during my first workshop with Ellyn, I was so overcome by anxiety about the changes to come that the risk-adverse part of me actually feared I might not survive. Clients have told me they felt the same thing, one needing to regularly reassure himself that though he might get hurt he knows he won't die.

Frightened as I was about shaking things up, I was even more fearful of remaining stuck in our old patterns and being perpetually unhappy. So despite the alarm bells going off in my brain and the voice in my head shouting *Turn back now!*, I decided to go against my natural instinct for self-preservation and step into the unknown, much as Julia and Mark did when they broke from their long-standing pattern of avoidance and began to talk openly about the state of their marriage. Mark said he'd assumed that once the truth was out on the table Julia would leave him, but even that began to seem preferable to how he felt each time he lied to her. Julia said that even though most of her friends thought she should get a divorce, she believed that there were enough good things in their marriage to warrant giving it their all. For once she was going to trust her gut instinct, she'd said. Even if in the end they chose to divorce, at least she would know that she'd done all she could. As therapy progressed, they saw that they'd greatly underestimated themselves and each other, both of them impressed by their mutual courage and grit.

Finding that grit in ourselves, mustering the courage to step into the unknown, will require that we tell ourselves a new story—one that is decidedly different from the one being told by our hypervigilant brain. Instead of discouraging messages of danger ahead, we need reassurance that no matter how anxious we feel, it's okay to keep going—that, in fact, it's *crucial* to keep going.

Rather than allow anxiety to control what we do, rather than avoid risk at all costs, we must find in ourselves an alternate voice: a voice to assure us that, dangerous as it is, we will live to tell about it. We need to remember that the growth and change we seek are more valuable than safety, that no matter the outcome, our risks will have been worth it and that we will benefit in the long run for having dared to take them.

The Takeaway:
Keep Your Anxiety from Running the Show

- When you're under pressure, nearly all of your emotional responses are shaped by your anxiety.

- Anxiety isn't going to go away in your relationship—or your life!—so avoiding it isn't realistic.

- You can learn to respond effectively to stressful and anxiety-producing situations in your relationship, even if your partner doesn't.

- 6 -

WHAT HAPPENS
ONCE YOU CALM DOWN?

Growing separately, together

We must be our own before we can be another's.
—RALPH WALDO EMERSON

"Tell me the truth," Patrick said as he cleared dishes from the table. "Do you think that I'm as pig-headed as Kate?"

Before I had time to decide how to respond, he'd already reached a conclusion. "I'll take your silence to mean 'yes,'" he said.

Our friends Kate and Max, with whom we had spent the evening, had been going at it about whether "a few" was more than, less than, or equal to "several," an issue that had, oddly enough, just been thoroughly debated by a couple in my office. Though Max was trying to make their banter seem playful, I could tell that both he and Kate were getting quite tense, as Kate grew increasingly forceful in her assertion that she was right, when, in fact, she was not.

111

"I'd be hard pressed to say whether you or Kate is the front-runner for stubbornness," I said, quickly adding that I appreciated his asking and that, in all honesty, as I'd watched Kate dig in her heels, I had been wondering the same thing about myself.

Several weeks later Patrick and I had a similar exchange. Over dinner he asked if I'd be willing to do him a favor. He'd spent the day in a coaching seminar where the participants had been told to identify three behaviors in themselves that they wanted to change. Based on the premise that awareness is a necessary first step in any change process, they had been instructed to invite five people who know them well to point out any time they were doing the offending behaviors and to say nothing other than "Thank you for telling me." Though two of the three behaviors he'd chosen weren't ones that I found particularly bothersome, the third one—blaming—was at the top of my list of good reasons to get a divorce. "I knew you'd be eager to help me with *that*," he said with a smile.

For years I'd been the lone advocate for change, exerting great effort to keep our fights within bounds. With practice, I'd learned to see trouble when it was a mere dot on the horizon, to redirect the conversation or take a breath and let go. I'd gained the good sense not to fire off the first volley or to fire back when Patrick shot first. And I'd made great strides toward keeping my anxiety from spiraling out of control when he would, for example, say I was being unreasonable when he was the one who was yelling—or, more challenging still, when he kept at it and I could barely resist jumping in. At first I couldn't really tell if my solo marriage-mending behaviors were having much of an effect. But eventually I realized that I was no longer the only one making an effort.

Now and again it was Patrick who took the role of the more levelheaded fighter, making the first move to de-escalate, biting his tongue or not taking my bait, looking at his part in the mess instead of scrutinizing mine. Like the time I came home to make lunch and all of his sandwich fixings were spread helter-skelter across the entire work surface: bread, mayonnaise, mustard, and two kinds of relish, along with the fork, knife, and crumb-speckled plate that he had abandoned.

"Hey!" I said, instantly irritated and not at all diplomatic. "I've got twenty minutes to make my lunch, eat it, and get back to work. Why should I have to spend five of them cleaning up after you?"

"You think this is good," he said, "to just walk in the door and go on the attack? For crying out loud!" he shouted—and we were off to the races.

"Why does my simple request have to turn into a fight?"

"Why do you have to make a big deal out of nothing?"

"How many times do we have to go through this?" I implored, about to give up.

I added something accusatory, and he said something snide in return. But then, as if he'd suddenly run out of batteries, he went mute. Rather than reiterate his position or ratchet it up the way he'd done each of the other ten million times we'd had this exact same fight, he took a deep breath and softened his stance.

"Okay," he said as he slowly exhaled. "It seems to me that

you're frustrated about two things. First I make my lunch and leave a mess on the counter, and then, when you complain about it, I get defensive and make the whole thing about you. Does that pretty well cover it?"

"Pretty much," I said, about to fall over.

He nodded. "I can see that." Then he began to clean up.

More and more frequently we had interactions like these, with one or both of us being uncharacteristically sane: approaching our conflicts with curiosity and openness instead of caution, generosity instead of rivalry. And each time, I was as startled as the time before, wondering what had happened to the old Patrick and Winifred, hoping against hope that they'd never come back.

WHEN YOUR PARTNER STARTS TO CHANGE, TOO

Given my graduate school training in family systems theory, I shouldn't have been all that surprised by the way things had progressed. One of the tenets of systems theory is that when you change one part of a system, the rest of the system will change in response. All parts of a system are interconnected and therefore interreactive. Whether we're talking about a marriage, a family, or a freshwater pond, cleaning up even one small part of the system will create the conditions for other parts to become healthier, too. It made perfect sense that as I was focused on changing the ways I handled myself in my marriage, Patrick was changing, too—without being asked.

To a great extent, I had given up thinking about the ways he would or should change. Or, more accurately, I had given up on being the general leading the charge. It had been quite some time since I'd delivered my last Sunday-morning lecture to him about couple development in general and our low level in particular. I offered no more pep talks about the joys of self-soothing or managing our own reactivity; no impassioned speeches about how if we had any hope at all of staying married he would have to shape up. My goal was to attend to myself and to somehow be able to accept Patrick "as is." Maybe that was the key. As I set my sights on my growth alone, he responded in kind: he stopped looking at the work he thought I needed to do and focused on his own work instead.

For much of our marriage Patrick and I had been so emotionally entangled that we might as well have been living in one skin. Every move that one of us made tugged at the other; every sigh or sharp tone or nasty retort tripped one or both of us up. We'd spent years in a state of defensiveness and hyper-reactivity, believing every one of our fights was meaningful and necessary, assuming that the intensity of our reactions was a sign that we "mattered" to each other, that we were still both feet in.

Tedious and tiring though they were, our fights were passionate. They had spirit and spark, and despite being unhealthy—which was no small matter—they made us feel connected. As we each became healthier, we bickered less and less often. Battles that at one time had seemed crucial to engage in or too compelling to pass up now seemed immature and trivial, if not self-indulgent. Words that had felt inflammatory or insulting became hardly worth comment. It was as if we couldn't bother to be bothered by the picky little nonsense that had sparked our struggles since day one.

Though this was in most ways a tremendous relief, this new state of being was also oddly unsettling. Somehow, in a way that seemed to have crept in unnoticed, Patrick and I had become surprisingly—if not a bit disconcertingly—*separate*.

There was me, there was Patrick, and there was space in between.

Sometimes I worried that our marriage was in a new kind of trouble: that we'd traded passion for passivity or indifference or, worse still, resignation. What if the reward for all our hard work was that we no longer cared?

At the same time, however, I felt charged and alive, delighted to have some room to maneuver without worrying about triggering some idiotic dispute or losing my cool. It seemed, at times, as though I'd acquired a superpower or a psychological bulletproof vest or had at last gained immunity to a bug that had previously leveled me. Some days, I'd have sworn that the actual space we lived in had become larger and more airy, as if we'd knocked out a wall or put in a skylight.

What had happened to the room with no oxygen, where I'd struggled in vain to keep a grip on my thoughts? And the inveterate scrappers who'd rather die than let go—what had happened to them?

What had happened, of course, was that step by tiny step Patrick and I had both been becoming more connected to ourselves—more able to tolerate and accept the ways we were different, more capable of calming down when our versions of reality or our opinions were worlds apart. Weird and unfamiliar though it was, we were at last growing up. And that growing, I discovered, had a lot to do with becoming more separate.

As I grew less and less reactive and steadier on my feet, I looked back at the many years of dizzying fights, puzzling at what it was that had made my thoughts spin in circles. *What could possibly have seemed so insurmountable?* I wondered. Was it the words Patrick would say or the look in his eye? Or perhaps the way that he stood or the tone of his voice? Sure, his fighting style was frustrating. He seemed to erupt over nothing, and once he got going, he couldn't let up. But then again, for most of our marriage, neither could I. But to have rendered me incapacitated?

For years I'd been so far inside the experience that I simply couldn't see out. But once I was able to step away from the action, it was much easier to recognize what had sent us over the edge. Having gained some perspective, I was able to see that when Patrick and I fought, I would be listening to his every word, while he was saying and doing whatever he could to throw me off track, turning himself into a moving target that would be impossible to hit.

Let's say we'd been discussing whether it was better to buy bananas when green or when ripe.

"The green ones don't bruise in the cart," I'd say.

"The ripe ones are ready to eat," he'd reply.

"Last week, we threw several away because nobody eats them with freckles," I'd counter. Soon after that, bananas would go by the wayside and everything would devolve, each of us becoming a caricature of our worst traits. Patrick would begin to sound like a sportscaster, commenting not on my previous comment but on the way I had made it. How bossy I sounded . . . how closed-minded I obviously was . . . how hypercritical I could be . . . what a terrible listener I was, reporting, in real time, just how frustrating and irritating he found me to be. In spite of all that, I'd be righteously trying to stick with bananas, green or ripe, clinging in vain to my senseless belief that our fights might be logical and containable, as if I were running an argument by *Robert's Rules of Order*. "Wait . . . wait!" I'd object, wishing I had a gavel. Meanwhile, Patrick would be going after the fine points of my personality and all that could be improved, bombarding me with everything he had until I was buried.

His strategy: criticize the commenter and ignore everything else. And mine? Try to make order out of chaos, even if it meant that I would die trying. I eventually realized that Patrick was just doing what he knew to survive and I was doing the same, both of us struggling to manage our mounting anxiety and doing a miserable job of it.

"Patrick and I are two peas in a pod," a friend of mine said when I described how illogical and overwhelming Patrick's strategy had been. "I *hate* to lose," he continued. "When I'm fighting with Annie it's a matter of pure survival for me. If I thought I was losing on bananas, I'd definitely try to win on character assassination."

Given what Patrick and I had each learned in childhood about conflict, we were bound to struggle in the ways that we did. Patrick's parents had fought, literally, with eating utensils and ultimately divorced. My parents had shoved all their interpersonal tension under the rug, taking most of it out on my brother and me. In both of our families, people went after each other acting more like inmates than loved ones, knowing only to defend their territory and watch their backs. What we knew about conflict was that it is inevitable, unstoppable, and dangerous. And that one should *never* back down. Even if you have no idea what you're fighting about. Even if you are desperately longing for peace.

It took getting some distance and becoming steadier inside before I was able to see any of this at all. And once I did, there was no turning back. Development is about growing and maturing, which means leaving behind old interactional patterns and outdated coping strategies, adding new skills, and becoming increasingly able to handle pressures that at one time would have been more than we could tolerate.

Today, I can barely imagine feeling debilitated by Patrick's anxious barrage, much the way I can no longer call up the feelings of terror I had listening to ghost stories in summer camp.

SO WHAT HAPPENS
AFTER THE TENSION DIES DOWN?

Ernest Hemingway once said that people go bankrupt in two ways: first gradually, then suddenly. The changes in my marriage felt exactly like that. As I had been gradually learning to steady myself (and apparently Patrick had been learning to steady himself as well), we had been slowly making our way up the developmental ladder, though I hadn't been thinking of it in those terms.

Then there we were at Stage Three—a stage of couple development I'd known about only in theory. Stage Three is *Exploration*, in which couples step away from the intense involvement of the two earlier stages, reconnect with their own interests, and shape goals for their own lives.

No longer needing to be reassured by sameness, no longer struggling to attain an elusive consensus, more able to accept differences (whether they like them or not), couples in this stage find themselves getting a lot less whipped up about the small stuff that once drove them nuts. As a result, they have more time and energy to do things other than fight.

Patrick, for example, began to make shifts in his work life, ultimately reinventing the entire focus of his business. He began reading for pleasure, not just for work, taking long Sunday bike rides and zealously studying to become fluent in Spanish. I decided to completely relandscape our garden, which meant learning about plants and irrigation and how to fend off the deer. At the same time, I enrolled in a series of short story writing classes and spent many evenings doing my homework alongside the kids. Often I'd be awake well past midnight, delighting as much in the silence and solitude as in the writing itself.

I, too, set new challenges for myself at work. Beyond the usual classes and conferences I'd attended year after year, I began to study with a new teacher, Dr. James Maddock, who at the time was a professor in the department of Family Social Science at the University of Minnesota. Jim was a pioneer in human sexuality and an expert in understanding the complex couple dynamics that we therapists must decipher. For ten years, into the very last weeks of his life, he and I would consult, by phone and each summer in person, about how to best work with my most difficult couples, with Jim consistently challenging me to sharpen my understanding and make bolder moves with my clients as well as in my own life.

Though Patrick and I were putting considerable energy into our own self-development, we were by no means estranged. We still ate family dinners and had date nights and took long walks together on weekends. Our time spent pursuing our own interests simply added a sense of breadth and balance that we'd both missed.

Still, there was a part of me that remained apprehensive about our new state of separateness. What if, one personal interest at a time, we were beginning to lead parallel lives—or worse, our lives were diverging and in time there would be no *we* left at all? Many of my clients have voiced similar concerns when they reach this stage, worried that the next thing they knew they'd be taking separate vacations, sleeping in separate bedrooms, or becoming one of those couples who take books to the restaurant when they go out to dinner. Some have said that, progress or not, they miss the drama and intensity their fights engendered, feeling that life has become disquietingly flat.

As is true at all stages of couple development, few of us pass from one stage to the next in perfect sync with our partner. This difference in timing can be particularly distressing when one person moves into Stage Three ahead of the other. As one partner begins to run marathons or spends hours practicing the cello or learning to quilt, the other will understandably feel neglected or forgotten, often complaining vociferously and demanding more time.

In a culture that glorifies togetherness, it can be hard to trust that being less entangled is actually a good thing. Having experienced it for myself, I've been able to reassure my clients that the independence of Stage Three is a way station, as opposed to a final destination. Eventually all this "me" time will give way to a renewed longing for connection as a couple, I say, adding the reminder that it won't happen immediately. Odd as it is, their separateness is likely a sign that they're growing, not a sign that they're growing apart.

PRESERVING BOTH THE *I* AND THE *WE*[1]

Years earlier, when I'd first introduced the idea that our marriage would get better if we weren't bound at the hip, Patrick was convinced that I was leading us down the road to divorce. Given our squabbling and the bad feelings it engendered, and given how guarded we already were, it made more sense to him that we should find ways to be close, rather than ways to be further apart. When I tell my clients that their struggles will ease up once they gain some psychological distance, that tolerating discord and separateness is a prerequisite to closeness, they're skeptical, too.

Most people think that feeling close and connected to one's partner is the cornerstone of a good marriage. They assume that closeness and happiness go hand in hand. Until I learned otherwise, I would have agreed. Intimacy and connection are essential (and sweet), but the closeness many couples seek is predicated on sameness. It is a merged *we-ness* like the one most couples experience in the early stages of their couplehood, a closeness that does not have the range and flexibility to embrace the reality of their differences. And it is this version of closeness that gets many couples into deep trouble.

The most stunning example of unhealthy closeness that I have ever encountered was in an interview with a young woman who had just been admitted to the psychiatric day treatment program where I was an intern. "Tell me about your family," I prompted. "Oh, my family!" she exclaimed, her face lit up with delight. "We're so, so close, it's like we're living inside a big ball of peanut butter, all rolled in together."

Every intimate relationship is influenced by the paired psychological crosscurrents of closeness and separateness that tug us in seemingly irreconcilable directions.[2] The first pulls for sameness and oneness, unity and alliance. It is the force that draws us together, making us a family unit or a couple, not simply unrelated people who happen to live together in one house. It's what defines the very important *we* in a relationship. The other is a force that pulls toward the separate, toward individual preference and self-definition, autonomy and self-direction—the part we think of as *I*.

Though few of us would question the wisdom of maintaining

both a *we* and an *I*, most of us tend more toward one than the other, while a healthy relationship requires that we have plenty of *both*. Too much togetherness will inhibit autonomy and prevent each individual from maintaining a well-defined self. Too much separateness will leave us disconnected and alienated, living like housemates or strangers or even enemies.

You might wonder: Is it an issue of finding the right proportions, like Goldilocks finding the chair that's just right? Or is it instead a matter of individual preference, with people working out what's right for them—some people wanting equal parts of closeness and autonomy, while for others it's more like forty-sixty or perhaps eighty-twenty?

Not exactly.

Managing closeness and separateness is not a matter of ratios and proportions, nor is it an issue of balance or personal preference. To quote my teacher Jim Maddock, "Healthy relationships require that we develop the capacity to be autonomous while at the same time be connected to, in love with, and close to our partner."[3] In other words, solid enough not to lose our shape under pressure yet open and receptive enough to express and receive love. This is the challenge we face in all of our intimate relationships: "to preserve both the 'I' and the 'we' without losing either when the going gets tough."[4]

For me, developing this capacity began with stepping out of the room during our fights, a practice that I repeated for nearly a year until I no longer needed the physical distance to keep hold of myself. Once I was secure in my psychological separateness, certain that I wouldn't get sucked back into the fray or sell out my own concerns, I found myself increasingly able to agree with some of Patrick's requests, better able to consider the world from his point of view in addition to mine. And to my surprise, I found myself liking him more and more.

Every day I see couples as they struggle with this dilemma, unable to disagree without feeling cut off or resentful, unable to agree without feeling coerced or fearing they'll turn into a doormat—couples stuck in Stage Two, still resisting their differences. Many people say it's easier to be a more solid *I* when apart; they can like what they like, want what they want, and think for themselves. Countless couples have said, for example, that it's much easier to parent the kids when the other is not home. The challenge begins when they get physically or emotionally near their partner—near their partner's wishes and feelings, their values and opinions. Then it can be quite difficult to be clear about what their separate self thinks and feels, no matter how strong and independent they believe themselves to be.

The psychologist Murray Bowen talked about how interpersonal anxiety is "contagious," how, when under pressure, it can be difficult for us to stay well-connected to ourselves. "Anxiety 'rubs off' on people," he said. "It is [easily] transmitted and absorbed without thinking."[5] He emphasized that our self-development and psychological health depend on our developing a strong enough immunity to our partner's anxiety that we don't need to distance ourselves or go back to "sameness" to maintain our equilibrium.

Many people admit that, given the high cost of dissent, they simply gave up the fight, choosing to sideline their own concerns in order to maintain harmony in their relationship. Clients have reported ceasing to read mystery novels because their partner found such books far too pedestrian, deciding not to pursue a career change lest they appear dilettantish, watching Red Sox games on the sly, saying they're off to the library to avoid their partner's eye rolling about sports. People have stopped eating foods they love, worn clothes they dislike, grown their hair long or worn it short, all because a partner preferred it that way. Someone I know claimed he'd gained weight, in part, because his wife found him "hotter" with love handles. And countless things people enjoy in sex have gone out the window without so much as a debate because their partner gasped at the mere mention of them.

The consequence is that people feel trapped and alienated and deeply dissatisfied with their lives when they push important aspects of themselves to the side. They let their dreams sink to the bottom of the priority list, along with their self-respect.

When I was first learning about couple development and introducing the concepts to my clients, I quickly realized that the terms *closeness* and *separateness* were easily misunderstood. When I talk about separateness, I'm not referring to physical distance, as in how many hours a day people work in separate offices or go alone to the gym or pout in two different rooms after a fight. People can be living on faraway continents and still have little or no capacity to sustain their autonomy. I've seen couples use all manner of distance to compensate for their inability to maintain their psychological space. They withdraw or shut down or bolt from the room, yet psychologically they're no further apart than two nested spoons. When I was twelve, a close friend's parents had a loud screaming fight that was followed by a full year of dead silence. They slept in separate bedrooms and assiduously (and dramatically) avoided all touch. When both parents were home, the tension level was high-voltage electric with wordless energy zipping back and forth between them—hardly an indication of any separateness whatsoever. There's a big difference between boundaries—the healthy defining of where we begin and end—and barriers that we erect out of self-protection or avoidance because our wobbly self is too easily influenced or overwhelmed by others.

When we are unable to stay whole under pressure, when we are unable to be psychologically separate, the best we can do is pull back, hoping to relieve the anxiety geographically that we cannot manage internally. I recall asking a friend of my son where he thought he might want to go to college. His quick reply: "Is there a university on Pluto?"

Maintaining psychological separateness is also not about achieving Zen-like detachment. There's no growth involved in telling yourself that you've risen above it when "it" still has you fit to be tied. No matter how much work we do on ourselves, no matter how solid and steady we become, no matter how enlightened we imagine ourselves, our partner will inevitably do something that knocks us off balance. Growth comes from getting closer to the things we find difficult, not further away from them.[6] We gain strength from learning to handle ourselves well under pressure, so that near or apart, we remain whole and solid within.

YOU CAN ASK FOR EVERYTHING—
BUT YOU ARE OWED NOTHING

In one of my early consultations with Jim Maddock, he made a statement that made me wonder if this whole business of becoming more separate wasn't suspect after all. I was telling him about a client who had a list of complaints about her husband that was a mile and a half long. Week after week she'd regale me with tales of poorly washed dishes, lost keys, agreements made and then ignored, speaking with an air of outrage and misery that I found difficult to take seriously.

"What you're looking at," Jim said, "is a person who believes she's entitled to have the spouse of her dreams, when she's not. None of us are. Remember, Winifred, we're not entitled to anything."

Nothing? I wondered.

"Of course, it's our job to ask," he added. "In fact, it's *healthy* to ask. After all, who else is going to advocate for your needs, if not you?"

My first instinct was to protest, to say, "Isn't that what partners do, they advocate for each other's needs?" But no sooner had I formed that thought than I realized how unrealistic that was and how silly I'd sound, given the struggles Patrick and I had faced, the two of us at times worn out and frustrated, barely able to advocate for ourselves, let alone for each other.

Even so, what Jim was telling me seemed sort of harsh. Part of me hoped that I'd misunderstood him.

Me: You say it's my job to ask—but are you saying I'm not likely to get it?

Jim: No, it's your job to ask, though you have no guarantee of getting it.

Me: By "not entitled to anything," you mean we don't get any guarantees?

Jim: Yes, because your partner is not obligated to do what you prefer—though it's possible that he'd do so out of his own generosity.

Me: So people aren't even required to be *nice* to each other?

I was growing even more dubious.

Jim: Being nice is optional, though I highly recommend it.

Me: What if someone's partner wants something ridiculous?

Jim: Ridiculous or not, we always have a choice whether to say yes or no.

Jim and I went back and forth for a good while as I peppered him with questions and he maintained his stance. In the end, I realized that he wasn't saying it's a dog-eat-dog world or that partners should run roughshod over each other's desires. His point was that it is vital that we ask for what we want from our partners because it gives us our best shot at having a satisfying and enjoyable life. But we must be ready to accept disappointment and to somehow meet our own emotional needs—to soothe our own hurts[7]—as there is no guarantee that our partner will comply with the requests that we've made. Recognizing and accepting that we're neither entitled to get what we want nor required to give what we're asked makes the whole matter of giving and getting far more of an adventure than I'd ever imagined.

This, too, is a prospect that can be hard to accept.

Most of us grow up believing that being in a committed partnership means having someone we can turn to when we need comfort and support. Someone we can wake in the night when we've had a bad dream or heard a strange noise. Someone who will bring us soup when we're sick, who'll make the phone call we dread, who'll trek downstairs one more time to check the back door: a person in our life who will make us feel cared for and loved.

As with most couples, the marriage vows that Patrick and I made grew out of beliefs much like these. We made a commitment to be loving and kind, to nurture our friendship and be steadfast through whatever difficulties we faced. In essence, to be there for each other, in good times and bad.

And for the most part we've done that—except when we haven't.

But any difficulty we've had living up to our vows hasn't come from laziness or lack of good intention. As partners, we've been there for each other as best we could. The problem came instead from the unquestioned assumption that each of us would be able to count on the other for emotional support the way we count on gravity to keep us from floating into the air. Hopeful and well intentioned as we were as newlyweds, it never occurred to us that a promise to be there for one's partner unequivocally is impossible to keep.

Many of us cling to the notion that a "good" partner is someone who won't let us down, even though not one of us has lived up to that standard ourselves. Better to be crestfallen or outraged by our partner's shortfall than to question our expectations. Better to think there's something wrong with our marriage or the person we picked than to face the unsettling truth that the support we get will be intermittent at best.

When clients first hear me question the sacrosanct notion that it's our partner's "job" to meet our needs, most of them look at me as if I'm making a joke.

"Are you kidding?" they ask. "What's a relationship for, if not that?"

For most people, it takes some time to grow comfortable with the idea of being responsible for comforting ourselves when we're disappointed or hurt and somewhat longer to discover its benefits. I'd recognized the importance of self-soothing back when my children were small and they needed to learn to settle themselves down for a nap or fall back to sleep at three a.m. without waking up the whole household. Applying that same concept to managing my disappointments with Patrick was one I hadn't considered.

"Most of us do not come into adulthood with the belief that we are responsible for tending to our own anxiety," says the psychologist Virginia Todd Holeman. "Instead, we adopt this formula: 'I'm anxious. You change.' Or we adhere to its twin, 'You're anxious, I'll change.' . . . Do these strategies work? Certainly. However, your emotional well-being now depends on someone else, which leaves you insecure and hypervigilant to changes in the other. You now have to control that person to maintain your peace of mind."[8]

It's better, I've discovered, to focus on controlling yourself.

Self-control is in part about anxiety management and all the skills that entails. But more significantly, it's about accepting responsibility for our own safety and well-being. It is the unilateral work of being our own source of support. Though it is by no means easy, with practice, many of us find that it is deeply rewarding and even empowering to quiet our own anxiety in the no-guarantees world in which we all live. When we're able to comfort ourselves and be calm in the face of possible disappointment, there's greater ease around our bids for our partner's support. If we can manage ourselves come what may, then, when our partners do respond to our request for support or connection, it can feel like a gift we are happy to receive, rather than a need we are desperate to have them fulfill.

But making this shift often requires that we examine some of our basic premises, beginning with what we really mean when we speak about needs.

What many people refer to as emotional needs are not needs at all, they're wants. Needs are the things we cannot live without—such as food, water and air, shelter from the elements, and a place to sleep. Wants are things that are optional—which is an important distinction in the context of our relationships.

When we claim that we need something, it couches our

wants and desires in a language that can be difficult for our partner to contest—as if having a need means that our partner is contractually obligated to do what we've asked.

When a person tells his or her partner, "You're not meeting my needs," the underlying message can be anything from "We're not having as much sex as I want" to "You don't make as much money as I'd hoped." It can be a way of saying "We're disconnected, and I think it's your fault" or "You're a terrible lover" or "I've stated my desires, and 'no' is not an acceptable response."

I once heard someone say "You're not meeting my needs" when her partner was no longer willing to stand in place and be yelled at. One man said it when referring to the fact that his wife had decided to let her hair go gray, claiming it reminded him painfully of his own aging. Almost always, it reveals an unquestioned belief: I'm not supposed to feel anxious, dissatisfied, alone, or let down.

Back in the late seventies, when I was first in graduate school, there was great focus on teaching our clients to ask for what they want. "Just ask," we'd instruct, as if asking were all that was needed. At the time, assertiveness training was in its heyday, and helping clients to speak up for themselves in their interactions with others was key.

But as valuable as it is to learn to self-advocate, the "just ask" approach had some serious shortcomings—one of them coming from the use of the word *just*. *Just* implied that the process is simple, as in "All you have to do is ask." *Just* made it sound as if getting what you want would, *of course*, be forthcoming, that it was our due reward for having had the gumption to speak up.

"Just ask" would have been far less problematic if we'd been told we might need a contingency plan. Missing from assertiveness training was its logical and necessary counterpart—disappointment training—without which few of us are truly equipped to advocate for ourselves.

Jim often said that the advanced work of marriage is learning to tolerate the disappointment you have in your partner and tolerating your partner's disappointment in you. Once we accept that disappointment is inevitable, that when turning to our partner there's always a chance that we'll be let down, we must then go about the business of acquiring whatever skills we need to be steady on our own—to be a separate and solid *I* in the context of our relationship. Life would have been so much easier for me if from the beginning of my marriage I'd known that I was the person I needed to count on to keep myself safe and calm.

Though some might complain that having to self-soothe is like winning the booby prize, for me, finally gaining this skill has been like winning the lottery. Having the ability to calm myself down in the face of disappointment, to take a stand when I must, has been far superior to being anxious or feeling helpless or angry the way I did in the past, when, in order to act, I needed agreement and reassurance from Patrick—when he was least able to offer it.

As we get better at soothing our own hurts and advocating for our own concerns, we enter a world of expanded options in which our actions are no longer limited by a need for our partner's approval or support; in which our steps can be bolder, our risks more daring. When we can comfort and encourage ourselves, we can choose our battles from a position of strength. We can decide with confidence what's worth fighting for and what we can let go.

And from this place of steadiness, many people find that they have much more to offer each other.

A HUNDRED PATHS THROUGH
THE WORLD THAT ARE EASIER THAN LOVING*

With all this talk about separateness, one might wonder, where does closeness come in? Clients have told me that at first they thought I didn't believe in closeness, that I was saying it's unhealthy for two people to be close, as if, instead of striving to connect, people should turn themselves into little islands of self-sufficiency and never have wants or desires. Some have worried, as I did, that separateness would only lead to more separateness, that by focusing on their own growth and development they would drift so far apart that there would be no turning back.

---

* From the Mary Oliver prose poem "March":
  There isn't anything in this world but mad love. Not in this world.
  No tame love, calm love, mild love, no so-so love. And, of course, no
  reasonable love. Also there are a hundred paths through the world
  that are easier than loving. But, who wants easier?
  Oliver, *White Pine: Poems and Prose Poems* (New York: Harcourt, 1993), 53.

As human beings we have a fundamental need for contact and connection. We long for physical touch and affection. We long to love and be loved. The promise of closeness—true closeness—was what kept me going through all the struggle-filled years. Yet the last thing I'd expected was that a deeper and more intimate connection with Patrick would be my reward for having developed the strength and stamina to be separate from him.

We need strength and stamina because intimacy isn't safe. Intimacy is, in fact, fraught with risk. As much as we wish for our intimate relationships to be an all-nurturing safe haven, unfortunately, they're not. When John Gottman, the marital researcher, spoke in Berkeley, he opened his lecture by confirming that fact. "Intimacy is dangerous," he said. Without a pause, 350 of us in the audience nodded in unison. *Of course* intimacy is dangerous. Though it may connect us deeply, though it may offer us moments of profound tenderness and love, it also leaves us vulnerable to hurt and rejection. It leaves us open to loss. And we cannot know when we step toward another person which one (or both) of these experiences we will get.

Relationships are a complex mix of sweetness and struggle, good intentions that are easily undermined by anxiety, generosity that comes into conflict with self-interest. At our best, we can be warm and comforting companions. We can create a refuge for each other; we can trust ourselves to let go. But no partner will always come from his or her best. What are we to do then?

Even couples therapists debate the answer to that question.

Some theorize that people can—and should—be taught to be the nurturing caregiver their spouse longs for, that partners should strive to compensate for the inevitable attachment injuries incurred in childhood. Others of us think that couples are far better off when they have the capacity to nurture and soothe themselves under pressure, when they can rely on their own inner resources and be their own source of comfort when their partner is not. Healthy relationships are ones in which partners can both lean on each other and stand on their own when need be.

Contrary to what most of us believe, intimacy is created unilaterally, as opposed to mutually. Intimacy comes about when one person makes a move to be closer to another, with no guarantee as to whether that move will be reciprocated. Intimacy is about knowing ourselves deeply—being intimate with ourselves—and allowing ourselves to be known by our partner. When seeking intimacy, we choose to step forward, daring to reveal ourselves—to be known come what may.[9]

Intimacy and connection between partners are also transitory.[10] They are experiences that occur from time to time, as opposed to being states that a couple attains and then maintains, like an airplane reaching its cruising altitude. At one time, I assumed that intimacy was a constant—a nirvanalike state that other couples achieved. In fact, I spent years feeling envious as I imagined all the lovey-dovey couples who were kept cozy and warm by their unwavering closeness, while Patrick and I would get chilly and out of sync and have to clamber our way back into connection. All along, I'd been thinking of closeness and separateness as opposites, when instead they are parts of a whole.

As Patrick and I continued our journey up the developmental ladder, I came to recognize how central a role closeness and separateness played in our growth. Every developmental stage is, in fact, about these paired issues; each stage poses a unique challenge in which matters of self in relation to other must be addressed. These issues are present from the very first days of courtship, when the focus is on joining, on creating the foundation for couplehood, establishing a *we*. What follows is the inevitable emergence of difference and the recognition that two people never truly become "one."

As couples, we grapple with the ongoing dilemma of how to be both close to and separate from our highly significant partner; how to remain our authentic selves within the relationship; how to be as connected to ourselves as we are to our spouse.[11]

The separateness that I had at first found worrisome proved, in the long run, to be invaluable. Our time spent pursuing our own interests, the work we each did to become stronger and healthier and more self-aware, were necessary stepping-stones to the deeper and more satisfying connection we would eventually achieve.

In the short run, however, I still wondered how we would get from point A to point B, how from this place of self-possession and coolness we would once more feel passion, or whether the best we could hope for was to be more skillful scrappers or to simply have the good sense to know when to back off. But sometimes I saw that the kind of marriage I'd hoped for was nearly within reach—a marriage in which we'd feel loving and connected and take pleasure in our friendship. A marriage with enough room for two. That was the marriage on which I set my sights, beyond the horizon though it was.

The Takeaway:
What Happens Once You Calm Down?

- When you stop trying to go through life hand in hand, you create room in your relationship that will lead to deeper connection—but not immediately.

- This can be scary. After all, if you're engaging through fighting and the fighting ends, what connects you now?

- Remember: one of the keys to having a strong, loving *we* is having a strong *I*.

7

THE BIG PICTURE

How to recognize what you're really fighting about

We see things not as they are, but as we are.
—ANONYMOUS

If you were to list every fight you've ever had with your spouse, you might be surprised to discover that there's a consistent theme—that your conflicts about money or sex or dividing the chores, regardless of the details, have a similar feel.

Most of us have the same fight over and over, whether we're frequent fighters or fight once in a blue moon. Our fights may seem to be different, but they rarely are. There's the fight about listening, about keeping your word, about losing your keys or your temper or your W-2. About being on time or pulling your weight. Or about fairness or honesty or the edgy tone in your voice. You may think you know what you're actually fighting about, but there's a good chance you don't.

Almost universally, couples are drawn into the content of

their arguments—who said what and why—even though it has surprisingly little to do with the real issues causing trouble in their marriage. When, for example, a couple fights about money, it may look as if they are bickering about whether to buy the expensive yogurt or the store brand, but their underlying conversation is about whether they are able to maintain their autonomy and still work as a team, whether they can trust and count on each other, whether they can successfully balance power and control. Whether we struggle with neatness or grumpiness or how to discipline kids, content is, at best, a great distraction. At worst, it impels us to fight about the wrong thing.

Entranced as we are by the content of our struggles, we are blinded to what's going on in the big picture of our marriage, as if we are focusing on a single blue square in a mosaic, never stepping back far enough to know if we're looking at a picture of the sea, the sky, or the wing of a jay in flight.

Taking that necessary step back, seeing the larger issues at play, is far more difficult than it might seem. The notion itself—that content is irrelevant—is a challenge all its own. If content doesn't matter, how do we address the seemingly important "little picture" issues that plague us every day: the teetering stacks of junk mail, the tax bill left unpaid? These issues are real, are they not? What about a spouse who humiliates his children, never answers her cell phone, or works ten-hour days and then some on the weekends? Or one who's defensive or nasty or goes silent for a week? If those aren't the real issues, what are? And how on earth can a person discern them?

Having spent years going in circles about Patrick's messiness and my dawdling and who was meaner to whom, I can attest that our squabbling resolved nothing at all. How could an argument about why the ketchup and relish were left out on the counter touch on the deeper and more significant issues that we needed to address—such as our mutual inability to tolerate criticism, our well-matched stubbornness, our shared fear of being seen as the one who's done something wrong? Until I was able to stop doing battle with Patrick over every piddling thing, I didn't stand a chance of seeing what we were actually fighting about. Nor could I have discovered what we needed to do about it.

How can any of us take steps to develop into a stronger, healthier partner when every bit of our attention is caught up in having our old, repetitive fight? In the midst of all that noise, it can be nearly impossible to figure out what our actual work is, much less identify the ways in which we're unclear or un-steady and begin to shore ourselves up.

HOW TO LISTEN THROUGH THE NOISE

In my early years as a therapist, it seemed beyond my ability to tune out a couple's story line and to focus instead on the dynamics between them. Resist as I might, I'd find myself all too quickly drawn into the drama and detail of their saga du jour:

"So we're pulling into the parking lot, and Liz shouts, 'Don't park over there!' Waving her arms like I was about to hit an old lady! 'What's the difference?' I say. 'Here, there. It's not like we're renting an apartment and signing a lease!' Then she starts sobbing . . ."

"You're kidding, right? You think I was *sobbing*?"

"Okay, fine, she starts *whining*. *For once*, she shouts, can't I just do what she asks? Like I'm some kind of jackass who never listens to anything! And I'm thinking 'Who's crazy here, me or her?'"

Tracking what was actually going on in a session like this was like trying to keep my eyes on an individual snowflake in a blizzard. *Why is she telling him where to park?* I might wonder. But then again, *What's it to him? And was she actually crying?* Quite often, I'd fall into the trap of trying to generate a solution, cheerfully suggesting, say, an agreement that the driver feel free to park wherever he or she wants—a seemingly reasonable move that would have no impact whatsoever. Sometimes I would contemplate the question about who was, in fact, crazy and include myself in the mix.

When I was first consulting about my cases with Jim, I was convinced that he was a mind reader or a clairvoyant. Where I saw brick walls, he miraculously saw windows. Just from my case notes, without ever laying eyes on my clients, he could see through the scrapping and the back-and-forth, the distractions and defenses, and the couple's litany of complaints. Like a heat-seeking missile, his attention would zero in on some particular line I'd written, some turn of phrase or emblematic interaction that I'd described.

It could be something as innocuous as "The woman said it's not fair." Or "The guy told me that, as far as he's concerned, there's nothing he can do to make his wife happy."

"There it is," Jim would say, his tone a mixture of delight and certainty.

"There *what* is?" I'd ask, having no idea what he'd picked out of my hodgepodge of notes.

"There, on page two, paragraph three, second line down: 'The guy thinks he's supposed to make his wife happy.'"

While I was still scrolling through my notes to find the exact line he'd referenced, Jim would proceed with a clear, concise explanation that might go something like this: "She thinks it's his job to make her happy, too. So they agree on that. Of course, he's going to keep failing at it because he can't make her happy. It's not his job. It's hers." Jim had a quiet and matter-of-fact tone that he'd use when pointing out life's existential truths, as if stating that the earth circles the sun. "She's going to keep blaming him because she doesn't know what else to do about her unhappiness. Right there's your work," he'd say. "To help them see the loop that they're caught in; to help her take ownership of her happiness and to help him recognize what's his job and what's not."

I'd have sent him four pages of notes, with details of each partner's childhood circumstances, their difficulties and losses, how long they'd been together, what their jobs were, how many children they had, if any, and the main reasons they'd both given for seeking couples therapy. Most times, I'd have included the particulars of some recent fight. Jim would skip over the fight and pick out a line like the husband's comment about his wife's happiness, and from there, we would construct our big-picture understanding of the couple's relationship system: its strengths and weaknesses, its binds and dead ends, the rules and agreements that governed it and the struggles those rules have engendered—an understanding without which I'd be as lost as they were, wandering in the maze of their small-picture analysis of what was happening in their marriage, trying to help them address the wrong thing.

Even now, despite my many years of experience, I can still become mesmerized by content and have to pull myself back. *You're losing track of the couple's system*, I calmly think, while a more frantic voice mounts its small-picture dissent: *But the guy's spending money like they've won the lottery!* Or *The wife is an iceberg and refuses to talk!* And although those things are true and serious indeed, were I to look at them in isolation I'd invariably lose sight of the dynamics between the partners. I'd overlook the meaning and impact of the overspending or the failure to engage and would then fail to do the most crucial part of my job: to help couples put their finger on the big-picture issues that run through their small-picture fights, to help them see and name their repetitive patterns and help each of them do what they need to get themselves unstuck.

THE RULES WE LIVE BY ARE OFTEN INVISIBLE

Everything a couple does makes perfect sense. Take the classic situation with a pursuing partner and her withdrawing spouse. The more she approaches, the more he withdraws. The more he withdraws, the more fiercely she pursues.

"We need to talk."

"Not if you're angry."

"I wouldn't be angry if you were willing to talk!"

Round and round they go, neither one able to envision a way out of the loop, both hoping it will be the partner's move that will put an end to their standoff. And though their dynamic may very well drive them mad, it runs like a well-oiled machine, each doing what's needed to keep the wheels going.

Yes, each partner can make choices about how to behave. In fact, lasting, positive change requires just that. But marriage is something greater than two separate people living under one roof. Marriage is an elaborately constructed system with its own rules and constraints, many of which we are only minimally aware of.

Just as the family you grew up in is a system with its roles and rules and patterns of interaction (never question your mother, keep a stiff upper lip), so is the relationship you've designed with your partner. Mind you, using the word *designed* can make this process seem much more conscious and intentional than it actually is—as if two people were sitting down with a paper and pencil and sketching out how they're going to run things. We create our relationship systems much more automatically and unconsciously than that. Sure, one of you might say, "I'd like to live by the ocean." Or "Let's have two children." Or "I'll shop if you cook, and then we'll both clean up." And the other might nod and say, "Sounds good to me."

But most of our relationship rules are negotiated behind the scenes, as it were, by processes of which we are not consciously aware. It's almost as if while you and your new sweetheart are sipping lattes and planning your first romantic weekend away together, your "people" are meeting with his "people," locked in some smoky back room cutting deals and negotiating the terms of your future together: *Okay, fine, they don't have to talk about sex, as long as he never brings up how often she calls her mother. And under no circumstances will she question how much he spends for his club-level seats at the ballpark.* Those terms, the agreements and rules you will live by, are based on an early assessment of what's going to maintain the stability of your relationship, carefully avoiding anything that might rock the boat or cause your partner to bail out. The terms that you stipulate (and those you reject) are heavily influenced by your anxieties and uncertainties, your unfinished business from childhood, the issues you want to avoid, and the experiences you hope to fend off—more than by your strengths or your best intentions for a healthy, growth-filled relationship.

More mind-boggling still: when your "people" and his shake hands across the bargaining table, the two of you have little idea what contracts have been signed. Unconscious or unspoken, those rules govern us nonetheless. They are the guidelines that regulate how we make our decisions and solve our problems, how we behave and how we express ourselves. They define what's off limits and what's open to renegotiation. And, no surprise, they shape the issues we fight about.

On Thanksgiving Day at Marjorie's house, there were, in her words, always two turkeys. One was organic, carefully seasoned, and slowly roasted in the oven. The other was Edward—

Marjorie's husband—who, at least from her point of view, spent much of the day steaming.

Even on an ordinary day, cooking together was fraught, as Edward tended to be a bit high strung in the kitchen, wanting everything they cooked to turn out as if it were being photographed for the cover of *Gourmet*. When cooking for guests, Edward became an out-and-out despot: yelling, throwing spoons, calling Marjorie names. When faced with this, Marjorie became anxious and servile, in an attempt to mollify Edward—a stance he detested and she hated as well but felt powerless to change. Marjorie complained about the drama, year in and year out, garnering great sympathy from most of her guests and every single one of her colleagues at work when they heard her report.

This year was no exception. No sooner had the two of them gotten situated in my office than Marjorie led with the particulars.

"Edward's outburst was perfectly on cue. As always: just as the guests arrived!" she lamented, her chin dropping to her chest. "I'd laid out a platter of cheese and crackers, some beautiful Greek olives, a plate of these little rolled-up zucchini—"

"Don't forget the pâté Leon brought us from Paris!" Edward gleefully added, as if the point of our meeting were to delight in the menu.

"Oh, yes." Marjorie patted Edward on the arm. "The pâté! My cousin Leon arrived with a slab of pâté," she raised her fingers up to demonstrate that it was a good two inches thick, "and . . . well . . . now I've gone completely off point," she trailed off, shaking her head.

"You were mentioning Edward's tantrum," I said impassively, noticing a brief sparkle in Edward's eye as I said the word *tantrum*. Edward was often tickled at being seen as a bit of a rascal.

"Yes," Marjorie resumed, "for once I'd like to join my guests for champagne, instead of being trapped in the kitchen while Edward has a meltdown about God knows what—the gravy, the stuffing, the fact that I don't mince parsley as well as Julia Child? All I wanted was to sit out in the garden and chat with our friends. Eat some of Leon's pâté. Enjoy myself—*for once!*"

"So why didn't you?"

"Why didn't I *what*?" she questioned, mystified. "Go outside? You think I could just leave him there—*alone*?"

"Why not?" I asked wide-eyed, trying to imagine the scene in the kitchen were she to walk out. What might Edward do? Throw the turkey out the window along with the gravy? Come after her with a carving knife?

Marjorie glanced briefly over at Edward before turning to me. "You're suggesting I could just walk out of the room. Just like that," she said evenly, in a tone that was both question and revelation.

Of course she could walk out of the room. She could do whatever she wanted. But I wasn't about to have the idea come from me.

"I'm not suggesting anything," I said. "I'm just asking what stopped you."

As if I didn't know what had stopped her. As if I hadn't stood in her exact shoes, riveted to the floor by my mistaken ideas about myself and my role as a wife—believing that if Patrick was upset, it was my job to stand by him. Or just stand there, period. Whether he was upset with me or not—but *especially* if his upset involved me. There I'd be, transfixed, no matter how circuitous or absurd the argument became, no matter how long it lasted or how late it grew, no matter how painful or unproductive it was.

"I can't possibly walk out. I think Edward *needs* me to be there," Marjorie pronounced.

"He does?" "I do?" Edward and I spoke simultaneously.

"What do you think he needs you to do?" I asked.

"I don't know. Hold his hand?" she speculated.

Really? I thought. Who holds hands with agitated men wielding meat cleavers?

Marjorie sat a long while, contemplating my question about Edward's ostensible need, twisting the wad of tissues she held into a shape that resembled a tornado.

"No, it's not that," she finally said, shooting Edward a contemptuous glance. "I think Edward just needs me to stand there to take his abuse."

"And you oblige," I added.

I'd hoped that in Marjorie's long silence she had begun to examine the meaning of that "obligation." I'd hoped she would look beyond the part of their dynamic that was about Edward and consider that the "need" she had referenced was actually hers. But by the way she sat tight-lipped, with her arms crossed, it was obvious that she wasn't yet ready to take that next step.

"Edward, of course, has a distinct part in this, too," I said, shifting the conversation to how the two of them had created this mess together. "He gets as much out of this dynamic as you."

"Really?" he said. "I don't think I get anything from this at all."

"You'd have to," I insisted. "You've been doing your half of this routine for years—in the kitchen and out," I added, knowing that his tendency to blow hadn't been confined to one room. "There has to be a payoff. Nobody does anything for which they derive absolutely no gain."

"Well," Marjorie said, fixing her eyes on Edward. "All *I* get is to stand in the kitchen, frantically trying to put out his emotional fire, when I could be out with my guests. What's the benefit in that?" she asked.

"You tell me," I challenged, prepared to wait out her answer.

YOU MAKE THE RULES FOR A REASON

We live out and are stuck with the system we designed—until we find it intolerable. But even then, it can be challenging to create the change we desire. One reason for this is that we're largely unaware of the rules and agreements we've ratified. Another is that systems are inherently resistant to change. Though systems are certainly capable of change, a system's drive for stability will be much greater than its interest in novelty (as in, we've done it this way forever; why mess with it now?). No matter how frustrating, absurd, or dysfunctional your patterns, changing them will require vision and grit.

So, painful as it was, on Thanksgiving, at countless dinner parties, before Wednesday suppers and Sunday breakfasts, Marjorie and Edward enacted their drama: Marjorie "stuck" doing something that she believed to be necessary (true for Edward, as well), all the while longing for change, unclear what form it might take, and questioning her ability to achieve it.

"The only benefit I can think of for staying in the kitchen is to shush Edward up. I'd hate for my guests to hear him being such a lout! Don't we all want other people to admire our spouse?" she asked, not expecting an answer.

"In all honesty," she reconsidered, "I feel just as trapped, guests or not. All Edward really has to do is raise his voice, and I tremble." She sighed, shaking her head. "I'm a grown woman, for God's sake! Why do I stand there when I so desperately want to go do something else? Anything else besides stand there feeling dreadful. What do I need—his endorsement? An escort? As if I can't decide what to do on my own.

"It's just silly," she concluded, dismissing it all with a hand wave.

To some extent she was right. It was silly—that she felt trapped, that she was afraid to let Edward work things out for himself when they went "wrong," that when faced with Edward's anxiety, she, too, ignited. But then again, it wasn't silly at all. Marjorie's stuckness made perfect sense, given the complex set of pushes and pulls, compacts and collusions that she and Edward had devised to make their marriage run. Silly or not, getting unstuck would not be as simple as Marjorie's hand wave might make it seem.

Before she'd be able to walk out of the kitchen and successfully handle whatever repercussions might follow, Marjorie would have to examine her own issues and do her own work: about her role as Edward's caretaker (and occasionally his whipping girl), about her long-standing avoidance of conflict, how as a child she'd played the role of the peacemaker and how she'd carried that into her marriage—with Edward more than happy for her to play that role with him. She would have to challenge her questionable notion that she was needed or even essential to Edward's emotional regulation, that without her he would reel frighteningly out of control. She'd need to trust herself to handle whatever he dished out and to consider, as well, the shame that she felt when others saw Edward in such an unflattering light. Hard as it was, she would have to write a new set of rules.

In the early years of her marriage, challenging Edward had been hardly worth the blowback it invited, hardly worth feeling intimidated or shunned. So, like most of us, Marjorie had implicitly agreed to a contract she would need to break in order to grow. But first she would have to read the fine print.

There she would find that she'd agreed to enact this humiliating exercise in exchange for security, for Edward's loyalty and love, ignoring the price that she paid in self-esteem, ignoring how, over time, it would cause her to distance herself from Edward in ways that would be destructive to both of them and their marriage. And, like it or not, she would need to accept that, at least for now, Edward had little interest in helping her rewrite the script.

Marjorie gathered her things and stepped toward the door. "How hard could change be?" She shrugged, her hand poised on the doorknob, before she and Edward walked out.

FIGURING OUT WHAT'S REALLY GOING ON

Understanding the big-picture meaning of our struggles can put things into perspective and explain behaviors and responses that would otherwise make no sense at all: Marjorie trapped in the kitchen and blaming Edward for keeping her there, Patrick and I arguing whether "I'll be there in a minute" is a literal term.

If you think for a moment about your biggest hot button, your perennial struggle, the fight you revisit and never resolve, what makes that issue so hot for you? What's fueling the intensity of your feelings, your reactions? How do you end up so anxious that at best you're ineffective and at worst you lash out or shut down or are fit to be tied?

For many of us, the answers to these questions don't come easily. When we ask ourselves, "What's *really* going on here?," we're likely to discover that we have no idea.

That's the point of identifying our big-picture dynamic: *to get an idea of what's going on*. Without that, we're walking around in the dark, bumping into our issues, wondering why our best efforts effect so little change.

The only way out of your repetitive struggle is to accurately name your patterns of interaction, to catch sight of them as they unfold, to be aware of the meaning you make of each other's actions and reactions, to recognize the binds you've set up for yourselves and the dilemmas you face—to see that you're locked into your frustrating, repetitive behaviors because the dilemmas you're trying to resolve with your partner are really ones you need to resolve yourself.

————

Cyrus and Ben had been dating for only six months, though they'd known each other for close to a year. Ben said they'd started slowly, as he was just coming out of a messy breakup and wanted to be sure that getting involved with Cyrus would be "worth the risk." Once he decided it was, what better way to celebrate their deepening commitment than to head off to Paris, the City of Love?

At first their days were romantic and their nights . . . even more so. The outdoor cafés. A moonlight cruise on the Seine. The Champs-Élysées lit by a thousand glittering lights. Then one morning, after a late night on the town, Cyrus woke up tired, grumpy, prickly at the thought of touch. Then Ben tugged Cyrus's arm as he headed for the shower, suggesting that he hurry up. "If you pick up the pace," he said brightly, "we might get ahead of the other two thousand people in line at the Louvre."

That's when Cyrus gave him "the look"—a stare so piercing it made Ben gasp. This was a side of Cyrus that he'd never seen. *Was it anger?* he wondered. *Or hurt, perhaps? Maybe it was more than that—something like contempt or even disgust.* But Ben couldn't tell. And Cyrus wouldn't say. The moment was chilling, and things worsened from there.

Fearful of a direct confrontation, Cyrus remained silent while his fury roiled inside. Throughout that day and into the evening, he kept his distance as Ben suggested in half a dozen ways—ranging from flirtatious to edgy—that they try to move on. But Cyrus was dug in. Ben had been pushy, bordering on rude, as Cyrus saw it, and letting it go would require an apology. He'd be willing to move on if Ben would apologize: own up to his part and admit he had been "wrong."

"But I didn't *feel* wrong," Ben explained weeks later as they sat in my office. "I kept wondering whether I should just say 'Fine, I was wrong' and get it over with. But in my heart . . . I knew that would be a mistake."

With no apology from Ben, their standoff continued. Ben felt pulled to meet Cyrus's demand, yet he was reluctant to comply, convinced that he'd be giving up a piece of his dignity if he did. Then, a day or two later, at the top of Montmartre, Cyrus took Ben's hand and the tension dispersed. But despite their good times, their ambling walks and candlelit meals, moments of friction kept popping up. An offending tone here, a raised eyebrow there, and the chilly edge of their struggle resurfaced and then vanished—leaving both of them weary and Ben mired in doubt, questioning if he really knew Cyrus at all.

WHAT ARE WE REALLY FIGHTING ABOUT, ANYWAY?

As I do with every new couple I see, I had begun to assess Ben and Cyrus from the moment we shook hands. As they told me their story, I watched: how they sat, who spoke first, the glances, the hesitations, the reassuring pats on the arm. At first my primary job is to listen and watch, asking questions at times, remaining silent at others, beginning to hypothesize and to test my hypotheses, seeking to determine the patterns of relating that they have built into their system.

Back and forth they went, retelling their versions, seeking a consensus that they were unlikely to reach. Cyrus explained that on that morning in Paris, he'd "made it perfectly clear" that he was exhausted. "Was that not enough?" he implored, the sharp edge in his voice sounding more insulted than angry or hurt. "I thought Ben was more respectful than that, more concerned about what matters to me. More concerned about *me!*"

As for Ben, he'd been hurt by Cyrus's harsh judgment. Punished by the ongoing silence, by Cyrus's chilly withdrawal. "Punished for what?" Ben threw up his hands. "The crime of the century: I asked him to hurry!" Ben went on to say that he was starting to worry that Cyrus wanted a "yes man," a role all too reminiscent of the one he'd played with his father. In the first months that he and Cyrus had been together, Cyrus had been attracted to his take-charge nature. Now it seemed that Cyrus wanted to call all the shots.

We talked about how they'd met, what they'd first been drawn to in each other, what they'd come to find irritating. And I introduced the notion of first disillusionment, every couple's first painful brush with disappointment after having seen each other as their near-perfect match.

Because they were such a new couple, together for less

than a year, their theme was fairly easy to spot. They'd had a dozen fights, tops, and all of them had come down to the same basic conflict: who had been wronged and who should apologize, each of them believing it was *he* who had been slighted or wrongly accused.

Why compete to be the more aggrieved party? I wondered. *Why all the focus on which one has erred?* Apparently theirs was a system with no room for mistakes, no room for the inevitable ways we fail to "be there" for each other, the ways we disappoint, misunderstand, or just want what we want. It seemed that the biggest "infraction" was failing to live up to each other's impossible ideal.

Most of us come into marriage poorly equipped to deal with disappointment and its painful counterpart: being the one who has disappointed our spouse. Until we develop the tolerance (and self-soothing) we need, most of us react to disappointment as if we've been dealt some grave injustice, as if we were entitled to have things as we prefer. And when our spouse is disappointed in us, we're more likely to insist that their disappointment is unwarranted, that we are innocent of any wrongdoing, than to accept that we cannot do and be all that our partner wants.

It's no surprise, then, that for so many of us, our struggles with disappointment show up in our fights.

This was a truth that both Cyrus and Ben resisted, each in his own way. And their fights about who was supposed to have carried the guidebook, who was pushy, overreacting, or insufficiently contrite, had them running in circles, leaving this piece of their big-picture puzzle unseen and unaddressed.

My questions for them, as we began to look deeper, were the ones I ask every client, no matter the issue: *Why this particular battle? What keeps you hooked? What's got you so locked in and reactive that you're unable to address the issues between you from a steadier place?*

For Ben it was Cyrus's "look" that had unsettled him the most. Every fight, from that moment forward, had been an attempt to "clear his good name"—to prove to Cyrus that he was a kind and decent person, that he was worthy of love. But nothing he did seemed to make much of a difference. Cyrus had remained stuck on how Ben had changed from the caring and generous Ben he'd first met. It was hard to move on from his strong sense that Ben no longer seemed loyal, that he could no longer be counted on. Every fight for him was a reaction to Ben being, in his words, "out for Ben."

"So what if Ben sometimes lets you down?" I asked. "What's the hard part in that?"

"And what if you don't always shine in Cyrus's eyes?" I asked Ben. "What would it take for you to still know you're okay?"

Initially, my questions seemed absurd. *What's a relationship for if not to get the things that you hope for, if not to be revered?* their puzzled looks seemed to ask. But as I unpacked their relationship through a long series of questions, repeatedly asking "If that, then what?," they discovered the issue that had been keeping them stuck.

"What if Cyrus no longer sees you as perfect?" I asked. "What if he claims that you're inconsiderate or unloving when you don't think you are? Let's say Ben doesn't always say 'yes' to everything you ask for? What do you take that to mean? And what if he doesn't have your back at all times? What then?"

Their answers led to the following conclusion: they both needed to completely rethink what they had defined as "love." Love was not about being flawless or dutiful or being someone's perfect match. Nor was it about being worthy enough to be given the things that you want. And every failure of empathy, every misstep, was not a reflection of their innate value or whether they mattered or had chosen the "right" man. Disappointment happens, for them and for all of us. Fighting about it was a battle they would both lose.

WHAT'S THE ALTERNATIVE?

If you think of your repetitive struggle as if it were a (not all that pleasant) room you enter again and again, the work is to pause at the threshold before stepping in.

What am I about to get into? you might ask yourself. *What's the alternative to just forging ahead?*

If you're having trouble answering those questions, you might want to think about your first fight and whether that fight is one you keep revisiting, either by content or by the feelings in you that the conflict evokes. Or you can just look at the last conflict you had. What set you off? How did you behave? Are you someone who takes a position and is unwilling to budge, or do you quickly throw up your hands or resentfully comply? Was the conflict over when it was over, or did you carry a grudge? If you look beyond the content, what can you see about you, your marriage, and what's really going on?

Chances are that some of your struggles are due to how challenging it is to accept and work with your differences. Every day I see partners each needing the other to want what they want, expecting the other to see the world as they do, insisting that things go the way they prefer.

But what if they don't? What if, in order to live with another, you can't be completely in charge? What does it mean to be the person who yields? How are you going to tolerate not always having your way? And are you willing to keep paying the price if you never let go?

It's possible, as well, that your struggles are fueled by old issues you've carried from childhood that are heavily influencing how you react in the present. Maybe the ways you were mistreated as a child—frightened or neglected or abused in some way—make it hard for you to trust your spouse, or anyone, for that matter. Maybe those hurts make you quick to flare or quick to shut down.

Fights can be easily sparked when the battles with your spouse replay the old battles you lost as a child, feeling, for example, that your point of view doesn't count or that you're seen as impractical or lazy or not very smart. Arguing in circles about whether you are or aren't being a lazy parent when you ask the kids to go play by themselves isn't going to address the wobbly, self-doubting place in you that needs to be shored up.

As you reconsider the question *What's really going here?*,

you may be starting to recognize some of the more trouble-some patterns that are keeping you stuck. Maybe you've realized that being withdrawn hurts your partner as much as her harsh words hurt you. Or that one of you needs to be right or to win every battle and the lack of trust and resentment that comes with having a winner and a loser is taking its toll.

In the coming chapters, I'll be showing you how to break out of your repetitive patterns. For now, the work is to simply identify one or two of the patterns that you find most destructive. *Here we are being overly polite because neither of us can directly express anger*, you might note. Or *Now we're into our thing about who isn't listening.* Or *Here we are criticizing each other for being too critical.*

Some clients have found it helpful to give names to their recurrent fights: "The other day we got into one of our 'I-was-waiting-for-you' arguments." "We just had another 'who's-the-boss' fight"—acknowledging that although the content may vary from one fight to the next, the theme (and unfortunately the outcome) is always the same.

For some, just saying "We're doing our thing" is enough to alert them to change course.

Calling your issue by its correct name is an essential first step, even if you're not sure what steps will follow. In order to design and then implement a strategy for change, you'll need to know exactly what it is that needs changing.

Here's the good news about working with your big-picture issues: though I've been talking about the interactional patterns that keep the two of you stuck, getting unstuck is not a two-person job. Yes, the two of you created your system. But, as you'll see, it takes only *one* of you to initiate change.

The patterns of interaction we create with our partners, the dilemmas we face, the rules we can and cannot live with, set a perfect stage for our growth. They offer countless opportunities for us to work (and rework and work some more) with the issues in our lives that are keeping us stuck. But first we have to see them. We embed in our system the big-picture issues we most need to master, and then we promptly get lost in our small-picture details.

That is, until we do otherwise.

<hr>

The Takeaway:
The Big Picture

- The content of our fights can be mesmerizing, but content only serves to distract us from what we really need to know.

- The key is to calm down enough to recognize your patterns of relating and give them a name. Then you'll know what to fix.

- No matter how stuck or frustrated you are, know that one person alone has the power to break long-standing patterns simply by doing something new.

<hr>

8

WE ALL PLAY A PART

You have more power than you think

Nothing so needs reforming as other people's habits.
—MARK TWAIN

My monthly case consultation with Jim took place on the first Wednesday of every month. By Sunday night, I'd have to decide which couple to present, allowing adequate time to send Jim my write-up, along with any questions or concerns that I had about the case. Most weeks I'd discover that after organizing my notes and describing, in detail, the couple's dynamics, I'd begin to catch sight of those hard-to-track big-picture pieces that had gone unconsidered.

I had been consulting with Jim for little more than a year when, one night, I began to think about Patrick and me. Let's say the two of us were my clients—what would I put into a write-up about us? Though at that point I was just a beginner at deciphering the big-picture issues of others, I'd grown increasingly aware of how little I understood about our own.

Trying as it was, tracking the complex patterns in my clients' marriages was a piece of cake compared to unscrambling my dynamics with Patrick. When looking at a couple in my office, I could watch what they did and how they reacted to each other and, with focus and effort, discern from those things the rules of their system. I could see their issues of trust, their fears of intimacy or commitment or speaking their minds: the big-picture patterns that locked them into place. But no amount of scrutiny or effort helped me to decipher the niggling and nit-picking of my squabbles with Patrick.

What *were* we doing? I'd continued to wonder. Yes, without a doubt we were conflict-indulgent—though, as we'd learned to unhook, we'd fought much less often and with far less gusto. For that I was grateful. But there were times that, despite all our efforts and all our growth, something would get set off between us and there we would be, back at square one, living through yet another episode of *That Old Issue*, as if the two of us had learned nothing at all.

There was no stepping out of the system we lived in. No bird's-eye view; no wide-angle lens. Those few feet of distance between my chair and my clients', the outsider's perspective that small distance afforded—there was no way I could get that, no matter how hard I tried. I fantasized about hiding a tape recorder under the dinner table or setting up a video camera as they do in reality shows—anything that might give me a fresh set of eyes on a world so familiar to me that I could not see beyond it, let alone deconstruct it.

I began to grow envious of the couples I worked with, longing for the kind of direction and guidance I could offer them but could not give myself. I felt like the cobbler's child, tripping barefoot through the complicated labyrinth of my own relationship, desperately wishing for someone to help us. There had to be *someone* out there whom we wouldn't bewilder, who would offer encouragement; someone with the wisdom and experience to look at our system and know what to do.

In the end there was; and that someone was Jim.

GETTING A BIRD'S-EYE VIEW

Jim and I had not met in person until the day Patrick and I walked into his office in St. Paul. Although we'd spent many dozens of hours on the phone poring over my cases, Jim and I had never directly discussed my marital struggles, and I'd never imagined myself as his client. I'd assumed he was off limits to us as a therapist. I figured that ethically, as my consultant, he'd be unable to shift roles. So I hadn't considered asking. But in terms of our ongoing growth as a couple, Patrick and I were, at best, at a standstill, with our repetitive struggles becoming more disheartening to me each time they occurred. By the time I reached out to Jim, I feared that the marriage I aspired to would be unattainable unless we got outside help.

Jim said he'd be happy to work with Patrick and me. In fact,

he encouraged it. Doing systemic work on one's own relationship is an essential part of training to be a couples therapist,
he said. He went on to explain that experiencing the process
firsthand, seeing the patterns we have with our own partners,
brings a depth of understanding that goes far beyond theory.
It's much like the difference between reading stories about the
ocean and feeling the cool salt spray in your face.

Jim met us at the door in a crisply pressed blue oxford shirt,
a navy blue tie, and khaki pants—an outfit I came to know as
his signature dress. He was taller, thinner, and more ministerial-
looking than the man I'd imagined. I had never seen a photo of
him. Those were the days before everyone googled everyone,
so I had to quickly reconcile the Jim in the room with the voice
I knew so well.

Once we were seated, Jim asked us why we had come. Patrick took a deep breath and began to speak. "Before I had children, I gave a good deal of thought to what kind of father I
wanted to be," he said. "I looked at my own father, and I knew I
wanted to be different from him. I wanted to be more involved
and more available to my kids. And I believe I've ended up
being the kind of father I set out to be. But as for myself as
a husband? To be quite honest, I didn't give much thought to
what kind of husband I wanted to be. And I can't say I've done
nearly as good a job as a husband as I did as a father."

Oh, I thought, utterly surprised. I'm not sure what I'd expected, but it certainly wasn't anything like what he'd just said.
In forty-five seconds, Patrick had come out with more honest
self-reflection and vulnerability than he had in all our previous

years of therapy combined. There were no complaints about how I'd dawdled that morning at the hotel or how grouchy I am when the house is a mess—the burning complaints he'd presented some ten years earlier in our first attempt at getting help. With this as a starting point, it was hard to imagine what might come next.

Patrick and I had flown halfway across the country to do what's known as a Couples Intensive, twelve hours of couples therapy spread out over three days. The first day the three of us were scheduled to meet from noon to five. The following two days would be much the same, pausing only to brew another pot of Jim's tea from Denmark or to walk down the hall to the bathroom. An intensive is different from weekly couples therapy in that the pace is much faster and the goal is specific: to send the couple home with a well-explained map of their system and some clearly defined goals for each person's continued development. Intensive therapy is big-picture work at its finest.

In keeping with the high bar that Patrick had set, both of us spoke about the way things had been going, with very little commentary about the things we disliked or what had driven us crazy about the other for the preceding twenty-plus years. Patrick talked about how he'd dug in his heels, and I fessed up to being chronically irritable and impatient with the ways we were stuck, admitting how quickly I'd throw up my hands at the first hint of conflict, primed to prove we'd made no progress whatsoever.

Jim took his time, asking how we'd met, what we'd first liked about each other, what had led us to marry, what had prompted us to have kids. We talked about sex and money, the things we fought about and the ways we made up. Jim took no notes during the session, but I could see his mind going as he compiled his data, constructing his internal schematic of the tangled system that we hoped he'd unsnarl, much the way I did when observing my clients.

Then, somewhere around the one-hour mark, Jim picked up the pace. Patrick had been talking about his emotionally unstable mother and how as a child he could leave for school in her good graces, only to find himself "in trouble" by the time he got home. He never knew what to expect as he went up the walk and had no idea what might or might not have influenced his change in status. I hated his mother for hurting him in that way, and I hated even more how it had set me up to be seen as one more woman who was "out to get him"—a belief that kept both of us stuck in a past we'd been helpless to exit.

Jim nodded a few times, mulling over Patrick's words as he gazed into his teacup. Patrick had garnered great sympathy from previous therapists about how dreadful an experience it had been to, in his words, "come through the back door" each day as a child and face who-knows-what from his mom. After listening intently, Jim looked up. "So," he said, carefully measuring his words, "if it was pretty much a crapshoot when you came in through the back door, I'm wondering if you'd ever considered coming in through the front?" Patrick and I laughed, but Jim was dead serious.

About ten minutes later he posed a similar question to me. I'd been telling the story of a fight Patrick and I had had some months earlier when I'd inadvertently disconnected the phone while Patrick was in the middle of a high-stakes conference call with new clients. In telling my story I had intended to point out how excessively bent out of shape Patrick can get, how punitive he can be, how he sees malice where there is none; but Jim had set his sights on *my* internal process instead.

"I knew heads were going to roll," I griped, describing my expectations of what would happen once Patrick's call was done and he'd come to find me waiting in the kitchen.

"If you knew heads were going to roll," Jim questioned, "why did you sit passively in the kitchen with your head on the chopping block?"

As opposed to what? I wondered. *Hiding under the couch?*

Until then I'd never considered that I had any alternatives (the most obvious of which would have been to offer an apology and then get on with my day). In two brief moves, Jim had made it clear that we had options neither of us had been aware of. His two directives, disguised as questions, highlighted how passive we were in the face of danger and how self-destructive we could be; how both of us were inclined to walk right into trouble, as if we had no other choice. I recognized immediately how unhealthy this behavior was and could even see where I'd learned it. But we had hours of work ahead of us before we would see that this shared course of action was, in fact, *central* to our ongoing struggles.

I'd had no idea how methodical Jim was, each move carefully timed and strategically placed. In retrospect, I can see that he'd been building a path for us to follow, laying it out one stepping-stone at a time—a path to a clearing with a vista, where our big-picture issues would finally be evident. From my perspective, it felt more like an amble with no set destination, the three of us meandering from this story to that. A little of Patrick's mother here, our circuitous fights there, pieces of one story joined randomly with the next.

Casual as our conversation seemed, far more had been going on than I realized. By midafternoon, something surprising had started to happen: issues that had enraged me, transactions that had left me feeling desperately trapped, started to lose their thunder, dimmed in intensity, faded by degrees from fiery red to a bland pastel.

Jim asked me to describe my nightmare scenario, to paint him a picture of exactly what hooked me in our repetitive fights. I chose my least favorite, though unfortunately most frequent argument: our getting-out-the-door dispute. In the middle of my story, when we got to the part where I'd go to-tally bananas over Patrick telling me, for the bazillionth time, that I take too long, that I'm inconsiderate, that I hang him up, that I'm inconsiderate (had I already said that?), Jim sat forward and put down his tea.

"So let me get this straight," he said, clearing his throat. "You do what you do . . . then Patrick does what he does . . . and then you freak out when he goes all *victimy*." His tone was just short of a stifled yawn, so intentionally blasé that it sucked the wind out of the whole ordeal.

"Precisely," I said. That's exactly what would happen. In the midst of a full-on attack, Patrick would claim that I'm mortally wounding him and then all hell would break loose. In most of our fights he'd insist he'd been ambushed—no matter what happened, no matter how nasty he got, no matter if he had started it. I was always seen as the sole villain. It was never both of us and absolutely *never* just him.

Of course I'd go nuts; who wouldn't? For years I'd been wondering how Patrick could think he was so helpless when he was standing there yelling. How could he see me as being so powerful, when inside I felt small and besieged, hardly able to tell up from down? As far as he was concerned, he was Bambi and I was Cruella de Vil. Beyond feeling dizzy, I wanted, ironically, to kill him. And that was the crazy loop we had yet to explore.

Given our childhoods, we were destined to struggle around power and powerlessness. Since day one, I'd been seeing Patrick as a force to be reckoned with, a titan of sorts, while he, in the meantime, held a similar distortion. He saw me as the all-powerful and overwhelming one, the one who was unreasonable and immovable, the one in his way. It made perfect sense that we'd both be ambivalent about power (our own and each other's) when the powerful figures in both of our childhoods had been unpredictable and aggressive. It was no surprise that we'd have trouble sorting our past feelings from our present facts.

Still, there had to be more to this go-round than our shared distortions of power—some way that my own issues had kept me tied into this web. And that was the piece Jim had fixed in his radar. True, Patrick was convinced that I rendered him powerless. And yes, my behaviors exasperated him no end. But *so what?*, Jim seemed to be pressing. *So what* if he blames all those feelings on me?

Jim had very little interest in my complaints about or grand insights into Patrick's role in all this. "We don't have to like what our partners do," I'd heard Jim say many times. "But it's our job to figure out how not to go nuts when they do it."

We were four hours into our session, and we'd cleared enough brush that all I needed to do at that point was look right in front of me to spot what had been eluding me for so long. "So what's your hook?" Jim asked softly, motioning with his hand for me to follow this all the way to its end.

Of course, I marveled, as the pieces came together. As a child in a violent household, I'd lived with real perpetrators, people who had done terrible things that truly hurt others, hurt me. And those people had been so frightening at times that now the slightest intimation that *I* was like *them* sent me reeling. I certainly had faults and could set Patrick off, and I could even be mean when pushed to the wall, but I wasn't them—no matter how Patrick saw me.

Patrick had his part in this dynamic as well. In his family, there was fierce competition for MVP—as in Most Victimized Party. There was safety in being seen as a victim. It was a source of sympathy and a way to get love, in an *oh-poor-you* kind of way. Above all else, being the victim positioned someone other than you as the bad guy, much the way claiming to be innocent of wrongdoing positioned Cyrus and Ben to still be worthy of love. In my family there had been no safety or sympathy to be gained from claiming victimhood. Each of us had simply run for cover in whatever way that we could.

In that magical way that the emotional baggage of one partner matches stunningly with the other's, the two of us shared one unfortunate issue that, seen or unseen, had kept us perpetually stuck: for both of us, the title of perpetrator was completely intolerable, and we would do anything, including hurt each other, if that's what it took to evade it.

WE ALL PLAY A PART

Most of us prefer to think that our relationship troubles are caused primarily by the things our partner does, when in truth, we *always* have a part in how things go. That's why Jim took no interest at all in my brilliant analysis of Patrick's role in our mess.

If you're like many of the couples I work with, you may be having some trouble accepting this idea. "What part could I possibly play in my partner's forgetfulness or stubbornness or short fuse with the kids?" you might ask. "What about when we have a small tiff and he looks at me with contempt or goes on the attack? How can any of those things be about me?"

Playing a part isn't the same thing as being at fault. We're not responsible for how our partner behaves. But let's say that when he digs in his heels, you dig yours in as well. Or, when he forgets to move the wet wash to the dryer, you take the role of chastising parent and he takes the role of incompetent child. Say, when he turns down your invitation for sex—twice in a row—you swear that hell will freeze over before you'll risk that sort of hurt again. At that point his issue has met your issue and you're one hundred percent in.

Remember, every relationship system is held together by its unique and complex set of connections—its spoken and unspoken rules, its conscious and unconscious patterns of relating. These interconnections between partners serve to link them within their relationship system, both people's issues fitting perfectly with the other's, two separate parts of a seat belt snapping together. A nagger will often marry a withdrawer, a liar will marry someone overly trusting or fearful of confrontation, a conflict-prone person will choose a partner who will refuse to back down. Linking, in the context of a couple's system, is another way of saying that our patterns persist because both of us repeat our well-practiced moves—even if the result makes us feel trapped. Even if we think we play no role whatsoever.

Couples don't stand a chance of breaking their patterns until they can see precisely how they've joined with their partner to keep those patterns going, much the way Cyrus and Ben needed to see that it was their shared inability to tolerate disappointment that had fueled all of their fights. Or how John and Celeste, the couple who fought nonstop in text messages, needed to see they were perpetually hooked because, desperate as they both were to have the last word, neither of them could resist pressing *Reply*.

The same was true for Patrick and me. We'd have remained stuck to this day if we had not recognized our ongoing competition regarding victims and perpetrators, how our mutual aversion to being seen as a perpetrator made it all the more likely that we would behave like one.

Working with Jim was an incredible gift. First as my teacher and then as my therapist, he showed me how to spot the exact way a couple is in cahoots and then find a way to present it to them that makes sense—thereby offering them their best shot at change. "Your job," he instructed, "is to show them how they're in the same boat; and their job is to find a way to get themselves out." In other words, my job was to clearly articulate how they were colluding to stay stuck and challenge each of them to figure out how to effectively break out of that stuckness.

One of the last suggestions Jim made to me before he died several years ago was that I hone my ability to succinctly state how each couple I worked with was exquisitely linked. "In one sentence," he'd added with a warm yet provocative tone— implying that the more concisely I could present it, the more likely it was to produce the traction needed to mobilize each partner to find a way out of their rut.

Was he kidding? One sentence? One *paragraph*, maybe. I'd tended to formulate ponderous constructions that, accurate or not, meandered around before hitting their mark. Jim's, on the other hand, would glide in like sleek and powerful birds that left onlookers breathless. Such as "Jane's afraid of sex, and Robert's afraid of Jane,"—his short and to-the-point comment to me about a couple I saw who'd had sex once on their honeymoon and then never again. Or regarding the couple who kept lying about their spending: "Both of them think they can buy whatever they want at no cost to their relationship." He'd suggest statements such as "The two of you had assumed that marriage would be a safe haven, when it's not." Or "The only thing wrong here is that you both think something's wrong."

His one-sentence comments about a couple's system weren't all so pithy or cleverly conceived, but without exception, they captured the unifying element that kept people locked "securely" in place.

IDENTIFYING YOUR PATTERNS IS THE FIRST STEP; CHANGING THEM COMES NEXT

Jim had a lot to say about victims and perpetrators, especially as it pertained to Patrick and me. It's not uncommon, he said, for people who were abused as children to think they'd done something wrong just because they'd been repeatedly punished. Likewise, they often had trouble accepting their own impulse to be hurtful or mean. The victim-perpetrator dynamic that characterized our struggles had held us so tightly we'd been unable to see it, let alone get ourselves free from it. Claims of victimhood, fears of aggression—our own or our partner's—along with the power and control battles we too often engaged in would do ongoing damage, Jim warned, unless we found ways to address them successfully.

After five hours of talking, we were all out of words. We'd covered as much ground as we could in a day and consumed enough tea to keep all three of us alert for a week. Through the high windows of Jim's office the day had gone quiet. The sun had all but disappeared behind a tall row of trees; the afternoon light was shifting gradually from orange to blue.

Jim had done just what I'd hoped: he'd listened and watched, prodded and challenged, and then right there, just beyond our story line, he was able to see the deeply embedded issues that held our system together. All of our craziness, our unfathomable loops, our painful reenactments—they made perfect sense to him.

But better still was the fact that, for the first time ever, they made complete sense to us.

That night, after leaving Jim's office, we strolled along the main street, slightly dazed, looking into shop windows, checking out various restaurants, and finally settling on a small, intimate Italian place that Jim had suggested. The maître d' led us to a cozy corner table, softly lit by a hanging copper lamp and a votive candle in a red glass jar. We stared at our menus, neither of us particularly hungry, both of us spent and grateful to be finally sitting together in silence.

Through the years, Patrick's hair had been gradually turning salt-and-pepper gray, but in the flickering candlelight it looked nearly silver, as if to emphasize the passage of time, as if to remind me how much we'd been through—how fiercely we'd hung on and how much we had changed. *You were kids when you met*, a gentle voice inside me said. *You were young and naive. But that's no longer true.*

It had been a long day, yet despite how tired I was, I felt surprisingly light, unencumbered. Gone was my sense of hopelessness, my desire to flee, the oppressive feeling of being held underwater, unable to surface. In its place was a feeling of space, of openness, of infinite possibility. Looking at Patrick across the table, I felt a tenderness for him that I hadn't known in years.

We sat quietly as the waiter filled our wineglasses and dusted our salads with freshly ground pepper. "Buon appetito," he said with a nod. Then, still with no words, we lifted our glasses to toast, and for a moment it was as if we'd just met; that the years behind us had gone dark and our life together was wide open, bright, yet to be lived. Except that this was far better than any first date; the richness of our history sat as a counterbalance to all of the unknown, steadying us like ballast in a ship as it heads out into open waters. We were anything but strangers, and though it took all of dinner and most of our walk back to the hotel, it finally dawned on me that the evening we'd spent—our candlelit dinner, the warmth between us, the way Patrick rested his hand atop mine, the way we laughed—had been nothing less than the yearned-for reunion of long-lost friends.

The Takeaway:
We All Play a Part

- When you get deeply entrenched in one pattern of relating to your spouse, it can seem like the only way for the two of you to interact. Fortunately, it's not.

- Recognizing your own part in the most troublesome dynamic in your relationship is the first step toward change.

- Playing a part is not the same thing as being at fault. Remember, relationships are a system and either your behaviors will keep things going status quo or you can—unilaterally—introduce change.

9

MARRIAGE IS A CHOICE

Making peace with the little
(and even big) things that drive us nuts

I love you no matter what you do,
but do you have to do so much of it?
—JEAN ILLSLEY CLARKE

Our second day with Jim began at nine in the morning and ended around one, leaving the afternoon free for us to walk the city and sit by the river and talk. Unlike the night before, when we'd eaten our dinner and collapsed into sleep, we were brimming with energy, feeling very much alive. As night fell, instead of going out to eat, we ordered room service, took a hot bath, and had the most passionate night together that we'd had in years.

For many people, the greatest casualty of the ongoing strife in their relationship is the impact it has on sex and desire. Many people find it hard to have sex with a person they're chronically mad at. It can seem impossible to feel passion for someone they find infuriating or to reach for connection across a chasm of estrangement. Who wants to open her heart to someone she barely likes? Many couples go through the motions of sex, having lifeless encounters in which their bodies show up, while the rest of their being is nowhere to be found. Others rarely touch, avoiding sex entirely.

And for many, their loss of intimacy is a deep, dark secret. That's why, when I first meet a couple, I inquire straight out, "How's sex?" Often they glance at each other and ask, "What sex?"

In courtship, before your first disillusionment, when the glass is always half full, before you struggle with money or chores or who left the lawn mower out in the rain, before you know he pouts when angry or lashes out in a hailstorm of rage or that she'll *never* be willing to have sex in the shower, never mind in the kitchen, that some things *won't* improve over time—before all that, having sex is, for many of us, a whole lot less complicated. Riding on feel-good brain chemistry, sex is what we do when we get into bed together at night and possibly again before our first cup of coffee in the morning. Sex is a way to say hello, good-bye, and all manner of things in between. Basking in mutual adoration, giddy with the infatuation of new love, sex in courtship is usually hotter and more intense than the sex couples have after many years of marriage.

Especially once their issues start driving them crazy.

Which is precisely what had happened with Patrick and me. We'd gone far beyond driving each other crazy; not only had we lost our passion, it was hard to imagine we'd ever regain it.

Even a warm good-night kiss seemed elusive at times. Having good sex after courtship, I eventually learned, is a function of two people being able to handle their insides far better than Patrick and I had been able to do. Good sex—or, even better, *great* sex—requires knowing what you want, being able to take risks without needing a guarantee of success, being able to handle the intensity of truly being close to another.[1] Patrick and I had been acting like children, blaming each other for feeling victimized, both of us hunkered down in our foxholes—a state hardly conducive to a night of hot sex.

With much of our baggage out of the way (or at least out in plain sight so we wouldn't keep stumbling over it), being together began to feel better and better. We were warm and affectionate, more readily forgiving, and certainly more generous. Even with the pressures of daily life, we found ways to sustain the depth of intimacy we'd rekindled at last.

Better still, our marriage felt *sane*. *We* felt sane. Not that our difficulties had up and vanished. Patrick was still messy, and I still complained about it. And he still put pressure on me to hurry up. We still tended to argue, but when we did, it had a far less negative impact than it had in the past. Conflict would happen, and it would be over. When we got stuck, we were better able to disentangle. Eventually, even my penchant for doing "just one more thing" before getting out the door or Patrick's habit of leaving his jacket (and travel mug, parking receipts, small piles of pocket change . . .) on the counter became easier to tolerate—at least, most of the time.

Ahh, I realized, we'd come to Stage Four, *Rapprochement*, when couples feel secure enough in their separateness, accepting enough of their differences, that they long for a deeper connection, they want to "turn towards."

But this step up in development, this new sense of sanity, of *normalcy*, did not arise simply from finding ways to address our big-picture dynamic. Early in our work with Jim, he had casually made comments about things in his marriage that irked him no end. Noel and her paper piles; Noel running late. Those seemingly offhand disclosures turned out to be an essential part of Jim's message about life with one's spouse. The first of them came after Patrick had said something about my being a nag (or, perhaps I'd said something about his being a slob). Either way, we were off and running, digressing into a brief volley of complaints served and promptly returned.

"You leave too much mess."

"You get on my case."

"Just put things away."

"Could you give it a rest?"

Jim let us go back and forth a bit, listening and nodding, looking from one to the other like a spectator at Wimbledon.

"I wish that Winifred could cut me some slack."

"I wish that Patrick would just pick up his stuff!"

"And I wish that my wife, Noel, would clean her papers off the dining room table!" Jim said, vigorously adding his gripe to the list.

Realizing the absurdity, I started to laugh. "The only time I get to see the surface of our dining room table is on Thanksgiving Day," Jim continued. "Not that it lasts," he said, his voice trailing off, and I imagined Noel's papers reappearing by magic, once again strewn hither and yon, when the clock struck midnight.

I'VE GOT SHOES, YOU'VE GOT SHOES

Jim had his set of teaching stories that he'd told to his students over the decades. They were stories we'd hear time and again—about Jim being prudent and Noel being a risk taker; how Jim sought order and Noel, adventure. Their ongoing squabbles about paper piles and being on time and her gripe about him being a stick in the mud. With every telling of their repetitive fight, Jim made it clear that such battles are not winnable, that we must simply stop protesting the nature of our dilemma. "There's no getting around it," he said many times. We all have our intrinsic conflict that we'll visit and revisit and never resolve.

Pickiness, dawdling, shoes in the hall. Once again I was reminded that it wasn't just us.

Listening to Jim's stories about his marriage to Noel was much like the experience I'd had years earlier with Ellyn, hearing her talk about her struggles with Pete. Before learning that they, too, had fantasized about murdering each other, I'd assumed that my fury and frustration meant I was failing at marriage. I'd thought that everyone else had discovered the formula for happiness. No doubt, other couples knew something that I did not.

It still astounds me how many of my clients expect that because I'm a couples therapist, I've got it all figured out. They assume that Patrick and I approach all our difficulties calmly and rationally (on the rare occasions we have them), that we always use I-statements, that we never get mad. Six or eight weeks after our weekend with Jim, Patrick and I had a rip-roaring blowout. A true barn burner, with "You're such an ass" followed by "Oh, drop dead."

"It's humbling," Jim said when I told him about it. "We go along doing so well, and then there it is again." He chuckled. "Makes you want to pause and appreciate the times when things go well."

Oh, I realized, *we never get "fixed." Nor does our marriage—at least, not in the way that we originally expect.*

I knew Jim was right, even though I found his message somewhat unsettling, even though some part of me wished he was wrong. Though I'd long since let go of expecting (and even needing) Patrick to change, apparently I still harbored the illusion that an ideal marriage existed, that at the top of the developmental ladder, up there at Stage Five, was a world of marital sunshine and blue skies. A world we could enter if we just did things right.

I began to wonder how many of my clients held that same belief.

Jim used to say that every couple comes into therapy for the wrong reason. "Once you convince them of that, your work is done," he said. The first time I heard that, I had no idea what he was talking about. *What constitutes a right reason?* I wondered. Is tripping over shoes in the dark a good enough reason? Or fighting about who started it or whose fault it is or who gets to have the last word? What about turning into a bumbling idiot with your spouse, while with everyone else in your life you're perfectly sane? Is that reason enough?

At first I'd thought that Jim was referring to the particular issues that prompted people to seek therapy—that there were both valid and invalid reasons for a couple to seek help. But in fact he was referencing the much deeper and more complex idea about people's mistaken ideas about who and what's wrong (as well as their beliefs about what will help make their marriage better).

In a culture that promises ten simple steps to accomplish anything, it makes sense that so many of us hold out hope that it's possible to have a trouble-free marriage; that there's a way to iron out all of our relationship wrinkles; that somehow, someday, our perpetual struggles will be resolved once and for all.

And when they're not? Much the way I did, most couples assume that they've taken a wrong turn.

WHY MARRIAGE IS A CHOICE

When Joanna and Luke came to see me, they admitted straight out that they were probably doomed. One day, seemingly out of the blue, Luke had woken up and announced to Joanna that he was no longer in love. There they were, ten years into marriage, with three children in preschool, Joanna working very, very part-time as a copywriter and Luke working seventy-hour weeks at a start-up. Life was hectic, they said, with work, the kids, socks and shoes and toys everywhere. All the little annoyances, Joanna's petty criticisms couched as suggestions, the way her voice rose at the ends of her sentences, Luke's never-ending succession of outlandish ideas—*Let's go live on a houseboat, let's live off the grid in Alaska, how about we start an ice cream shop after the company IPOs?*—were doubly annoying since there wasn't enough good stuff to balance them out. Then Luke "drove the final nail into the coffin," as Joanna saw it, telling her he loved her but was no longer in love.

Joanna's friends were sharply divided, a few telling her to just see what happened, to take it slow, while others started sending her the names of divorce mediators, saying that if Luke didn't love her, there wasn't much she could do. "There are plenty of guys out there who would think you're a great catch," one friend said by way of encouragement. Another advised, "Don't sit around waiting for crumbs."

Then there was Luke's therapist opining that "maybe Joanna just isn't the woman for you," as if Luke had been deciding whether he and Joanna should or shouldn't go on a third date. But Joanna still loved Luke and wasn't ready to leave, and all the conflicting advice was only making matters worse.

By the time they showed up in my office, Luke had begun to rethink his pronouncement about not being in love. Maybe he'd overstated his feelings. Maybe things weren't that bad. Not that he'd begun to see shooting stars when Joanna walked into the room, but maybe his "I'm not in love" comment was his way of saying that there were problems in the marriage and he'd been too busy to notice his unhappiness until it was all that he felt.

"How far is too far gone?" they asked, saying that it seemed to them that staying married when you're not really happy had gone out of vogue. *How happy is happy enough to stay?*

As I began to take in Jim's message about how distressed we can become when we expect marriage to be one blissful day leading into the next, I thought about the books I had read (and had been discouraged by) early on in my marriage, the ones with the pictures of smiling couples on the cover, the ones promising to turn all your conflicts into joyful opportunities. Those books were perpetuating a dangerous myth, setting so high and unrealistic a bar that it made struggling couples want to give up.

Then I thought about my comparatively sober message to clients about the bumpy road of marriage, about the need to tolerate frustration and disappointment, about the need to take bold steps on their own if they wanted to grow (the very message I gave Joanna and Luke, assuring them that the problems in their marriage were hardly cause to give up).

With all that, I already felt as though I were telling my clients that there isn't a tooth fairy.

Now I would have to go one step further, deliver one more piece of bad news: I would have to tell them that some of their most frustrating struggles would never resolve. I would have to say that in order to grow, they'd need to find a way to accept this, to let go of believing that it can be otherwise. To trust that letting go will open doors to a better marriage rather than close them.

How could I say this to someone hopeless and desperate, intractably stuck in a miserable marriage, barely hanging on to the end of her rope? I thought of my client whose wife had only two volumes: yelling loud enough for the neighbors to hear or saying nothing at all. And of the woman whose husband drank vodka from a travel mug as he drove home from work.

What should I tell them?

Eventually I realized that I would have to tell them the truth.

If I had any hope at all of helping my clients, no matter how dire their troubles, I had to remind them that marriage is a choice. We can stay with our partner, or we can leave. If we stay, we have to figure out how to navigate the difficult waters of our marriage. We have to stop protesting the nature of whatever dilemma we face. We have to find a way to have staying be a choice we make wholeheartedly—a choice we make without compromising the self we've worked so hard to strengthen.

But before I could do that, before I could tell them the truth, I'd need to accept it myself.

MARRIAGE GETS BETTER WHEN WE GET BETTER

I left our weekend with Jim the way I'd left that first workshop with Ellyn: with no detailed road map or clear set of directions. Just a YOU ARE HERE marker and a desired destination. We'd finally given our issue its correct name. But as for how to free ourselves from our long-standing struggle, how to call a cease-fire in our battle—Jim had left that in our hands, charging each of us with the task of figuring it out for ourselves.

Really? I thought, having, in all honesty, assumed that he would tell us just what to do. I had gone to Jim with the same expectation my clients have when they come to see me. They come looking for answers, hoping I can tell them exactly what steps to take to get out of their quandary, as if there's a ready-made answer, a one-size-fits-all solution that will resolve the unique dilemma that they face with their partner. They ask, "What should we do?," as if my telling them how to grow would be enough to enable their growing.

What I offer, instead, is what Jim offered us: a clear under-standing of the ways we were stuck and an invitation to seek our own solutions, to do our own exploring, to connect with the strong and solid parts in ourselves that, if we listen closely, will point the way.

On the plane ride home, I began to envision my next steps, with several key thoughts in mind. There was a way for me to step off the hamster wheel of our big-picture struggles, and it was my job to discover it. Doing so would require that I keep in mind the unwinnable battle I was repeatedly fight-ing. I would have to stop fighting that battle, no matter how compelling it was.

Though we'd built our system together, it was now up to each of us to free ourselves in our own way. Yes, this was our shared systemic construction—complete with its power and control battles and penchant for blame—but in order to deconstruct it, to make the changes I envisioned, I had to be willing to attend to my part alone. Getting unstuck, having the kind of marriage I longed for, would require that I focus more on changing my response to our struggles and less (or not at all) on my frustration about having those struggles in the first place.

Once I came to accept that the work of marriage is ongoing, that there's no "miracle cure," a surprising thing happened.

It turns out that once we stop having grass-is-greener fantasies and stop bemoaning our fate, we can get busy trying to make happen what matters to us, what will have the greatest chance of making a difference. We can work to unhook ourselves from our repetitive struggles. We can challenge the rules that we've allowed to constrain us.

When we do, marriage really does get better. And not just a resigned, suck-it-up kind of better. It gets better in a quieted-down, no-need-to-freak-out, tolerant, resilient, I'm-okay kind of way. It gets better because we realize we have choices—choices that we ourselves have made possible.

We're not just running on automatic.

We're not just following the rules or complaining about the rules we're unable to challenge or change.

Marriage gets better because *we* get better. Healthier. Steadier. More prepared to do what marriage really requires. More prepared to go about the business of learning how best to be married to the exasperating, lovable partner we picked.

The Takeaway:

Marriage Is a Choice

- Choosing to stay in your marriage is a decision you make every day, through good times and bad.

- Every relationship comes with its unique set of challenges and dilemmas. We don't have to like the distressing parts, but we do have to figure out how we want to handle them.

- Marriage gets better when we get better at doing the challenging work it requires.

10

HIDDEN IN PLAIN SIGHT

How we get unhooked from our big-picture issues

That's the way things come clear. All of a sudden.
And then you realize how obvious they've been all along.
—MADELEINE L'ENGLE

A few weeks after we'd gotten back from our intensive, Patrick and I found ourselves teetering on the brink of one of our perennial battles: Ms. Slow-to-Get-Going vs. Mr. Let's-Hurry-Up.

That day, like most Sundays, we had made plans to go out for an afternoon walk. Nearly every Sunday, unless it's pouring rain, Patrick and I make it a priority to head out together for a long, strenuous walk. In many ways we've considered it a highlight of our week—viewing it much like a date, both of us valuing the opportunity to be out together doing something we love.

But this highly enjoyable event has also been the occasion for run-ins with our hardest-to-embrace differences. Getting out the door for our walk is a perfect setup for my dawdler to clash with Patrick's scheduler—and until we discovered an alternative, we often left the house quarreling.

"I'd just like to point out that it's three thirty-seven."

"I'd just like to point out that you're starting a fight."

"How it can take twenty-two minutes for one person to put on her shoes and walk out the door?"

"What's the difference? It's Sunday. We're not catching a train."

Each week was the same as the last—as if our interaction were scripted, as if the outcome were inevitable. As if I could in no way speed up and he couldn't possibly relax. You'd think from our fluster that we'd not seen it coming or we assumed ourselves utterly helpless to stop it. Many couples I see do the very same thing: they approach some familiar old relationship pothole, pause for a moment to peer into its depths, and, as if succumbing to gravity, fall into it headlong. As couples, our systemic patterns are often more powerful than our ability to interrupt them, so again and again we're sucked into these go-rounds, playing our wearisome parts until we gain the skills to do otherwise.

Armed with the commitment I'd made to myself after our intensive, on this particular Sunday I was determined to do something new and improved. But true to form, I "lost track of time," and when Patrick asked if I was ready to walk, my answer was, sadly, no. First I couldn't find my sunglasses, then I needed my keys, and after that I needed to pee, so by the time we made it down the front steps, we were already doomed. No sooner had we turned left at the driveway than, as if on cue,

Patrick launched into his predictable litany: "Why in the world does it take you so long?" he moaned. "Can't we just set a time and stick to it?"

"Let's just walk," I replied, hoping we wouldn't spend the entire time squabbling about my tardiness the way we so often did. Hoping that I had the wherewithal to resist firing off some combative remark.

"It's nice out," I said brightly, aiming to steer us toward a sunnier start.

"I could have been reading a book or writing an email," he grumbled.

"Let's just walk," I repeated, already doubting my stamina.

"You *know* how much I hate waiting around. I find you incredibly inconsiderate. It's not like it's *impossible* for a person to be on time."

"Let's just walk," I said, feeling wobblier still.

Any two people can work out any issue if they want to, I told myself over and over, using one of Jim's phrases as a steadying mantra. When that started to fail, I switched to internally repeating *I think I can, I think I can . . .*

Patrick kept tossing out bait, and I soon found myself digging my front teeth into my lip.

Proceeding in silence, I thought of a dozen things I could say out loud, but I was certain that every one of them would add fuel to the fire. If I said I was sorry, Patrick was likely to scoff. If I suggested he drop it, he'd hear that as dismissive and then think that I didn't care about his concerns. I couldn't promise that I would never be late again, because I don't like to lie.

Silence was my best course of action, but it was understandably pissing him off. Even so, it was the most prudent alternative I had.

For some, silence would be a step backward, as their growth move would be to muster the courage to speak up. Not for me. My commitment was to do something new, to effect a different outcome to our miserable and tedious argument. Silence was clearly a healthy and necessary first step. Keeping in mind that the definition of insanity is doing the same thing over and over again and expecting different results, I was determined to find a way to be sane.

Did I have a plan? Had I thought this out in advance? Not at all. I had only one thing in mind: a commitment to do something new, which, at first, meant *not* doing what I usually did.

So up the hill we went, Patrick grudgingly silent for stretches and then revving up in the hope of pulling me into our familiar morass.

"Now you're giving me the silent treatment?" he groused at one point.

"Very mature!" he said a few moments later.

We'd walked two miles straight uphill at a brisk pace, and though he'd continued to grumble, technically we were not in a fight because I was not stepping into the ring.

"Look," I finally said, turning to face him. "As much as you hate my dawdling, I hate fighting about it. I'm being quiet because everything I can think of to say will just make things worse."

Everything, that is, except what I'd just said.

Patrick opened his mouth to speak and then apparently thought better of it. With a brief nod and a hand motion that said *Okay, carry on*, he stopped hounding me and the two of us made our way, wordlessly, up to our usual turnaround point, a small park with a breathtaking view of the Golden Gate Bridge. Climbing in silence, I had time to reflect, and I saw how our "get-out-the-door" fight was a prime example of the dynamic we'd worked on with Jim—the victim-perpetrator struggle that we'd been caught in for years.

Patrick's position was that I was inconsiderate and wrong, and when he harangued me I thought much the same about him. I saw how both of us wanted the other to provide relief from our gridlock and that we both believed we were innocent when neither of us was.

"The victim-perpetrator dynamic is always destructive," I eventually said, placing a gentle hand on Patrick's arm. His only response was a slow nod of agreement. This, too, was a refreshing departure from our timeworn struggle.

So that's how it works. I smiled, delighted to have, at last, blazed a new trail.

SLOWLY, THEN ALL AT ONCE

Change happens just like that. Like a patch of blue sky breaking through the dark cloud cover after days and days of relentless rain. We have a new thought, a good idea, a fresh take on an old situation that opens the way for something new to occur.

When people report change, they often say things such as:

"We were in the middle of doing our same old thing, and suddenly it occurred to me . . ."

"I was just about to cry like I always do, and then I thought, *What am I doing? This is ridiculous! Why am I letting him get to me like this?*"

"Greg made some nasty crack, and I was about to dish it right back, but instead I asked myself, *How many more years do we have left? Do I want to spend them acting like this?*"

"I have no idea why, but I just started to laugh."

"Something came over me, and I said to myself, *Now's your chance. Speak up.*"

Alternatives are everywhere, and so are solutions, though when we're deep in our rut we're rarely able to spot them. We bumble around in our familiar struggles, turning to our old, ineffective strategies, responding in ways that are predictably unsatisfying. And then one day there it is, a new path right at our feet, as if it had been hidden in plain sight and then suddenly revealed to us. Our thought: "I'm amazed that I never saw this before!"

It can seem as if change has come out of nowhere, when, in fact, it is a result of concerted hard work. Change in a marriage doesn't happen magically. We envision the change we want, and then, step-by-step, we become someone who is capable of making that change. We fall seven times and we stand up eight, growing more solid and sure with each step and stumble. We get lost, take wrong turns, and have to retrace our steps, all the while discovering what moves us toward our goals and what sets us back; what keeps us living smaller than we wish; and what brings us deeper satisfaction and a better life with our spouse. With patience and perseverance and a keen eye on ourselves, we see what it is that we do to keep ourselves stuck, and we develop the strength to take actions that free us.

Roger and Sharon lived in a world of self-protection, each viewing the other as someone who was more a source of danger than comfort. Neither of them was able to see the negative impact of their own actions, nor could they see the loving things they might do to ease the wariness between them. The best they could do was try to limit the other's negative impact. The first time I met them I thought, *Here are two basically decent people who are so afraid to be vulnerable that they behave in ways that practically guarantee that the other won't get anywhere near them.*

Sharon would regularly say things such as "Why did you put the salt in the cupboard when you know I like it left on the counter?," as if Roger had done it just to annoy her. "Why did you give me that look?" "Why did you use the word *condiments*? Why didn't you just say *ketchup and mustard*?" At least once a day she'd tell Roger that he was disrespectful, unkind, that he'd done something to hurt her feelings, that he'd done something wrong.

Roger would say things such as "I don't think there's anything wrong with the word *condiment*." "Why are you always picking on me?" Then he'd throw up his hands, grumble about

Sharon being impossible to live with, and walk out of the room, muttering expletives as he made his retreat. At least once a day he would go to his study, first slamming and then locking the door.

As a therapist it can be all too easy to take sides, to think, *Poor Roger. How can he stand it? If I was married to Sharon, I'd slam the door, too.* As a reader, you might think the same thing. You might be asking *Why should Roger have to put up with Sharon's never-ending criticism?* You might be in Roger's position yourself.

Or you might be Sharon, married to someone who, from your point of view, doesn't care how you feel or has little or no interest in listening to what you have to say. You might be thinking *Why does he treat me so badly? All he does is defend himself. Why is he always shutting me out?*

When it comes to marriage, there are no sides. Yes, some marriages are truly awful. Some people behave in abominable ways. Even so, keep in mind that marriage is a system, made of individual parts all working together to maintain the status quo, healthy or otherwise. Though its parts interlock, a relationship system isn't Fort Knox. At any time, one partner can make a unilateral move. And one move is all that it takes to disrupt the systemic pattern, to introduce change.

I often use the metaphor of a one-lane bridge where two cars are nose to nose in the middle. One car will have to move; there's no way around it, unless they want to sit there for all of eternity. Which, unfortunately, many couples will do. They'll remain at an impasse out on that bridge, each one waiting and waiting for the other to back up. Waiting for the other to resolve whatever dilemma they've been unable to resolve.

Who will move first? What move will they make? I'm always curious to see.

Let's say it's Sharon who decides to make the first move. She might start by recognizing that her running commentary on Roger's behavior is contributing to the climate of hostility that she finds deeply upsetting. If she wants to feel closer to Roger, she'll need to stop pushing him away. She might question why she's so intolerant of Roger's word choice, the way he tucks in the bedcovers, the way he breathes when he eats. She might try to make sense of why she's so easily offended. What might happen if she lets down her defenses, if she stops trying to fend Roger off?

Then again, Roger could change his role in their dynamic. He could quit pleading his case, defending his innocence, arguing with Sharon about his merits as a spouse. He could recognize that Sharon's control moves are due to her tremendous anxiety, her lack of resilience, her tendency to think that Roger is either trying to make her miserable or doesn't care enough about her or her needs. He could stop taking her anxious accusations personally, which might leave some room for him to be gentle instead of harsh. He could stop believing, deep down, that with regard to his being inconsiderate and hurtful, Sharon is right.

As it turned out, it was Roger who moved first, in a way that surprised him as much as it surprised me. Roger moved in a quantum leap sort of way, going from believing he had no options whatsoever to forging boldly ahead.

He and Sharon had been engaged in one of their typical upsets, with Roger telling her that the noisy, messy job of having the roof repaired was going to take an additional day. This meant that the workmen would be pounding away when Sharon's monthly book group was to meet at their house, though two days earlier, he'd promised that they would be done. Sharon was disappointed and angry, just as Roger had expected. Then she went one step further and blamed Roger for being deceptive, for not having thought of the inconvenience to her, for not having insisted that the roofers complete the job on time.

"I'm not sure I can continue in a marriage like this," she said.

That's when Roger said something inside of him snapped. But instead of being flooded with anxiety and then lashing out, he was flooded with calm.

"Sharon," he said, after taking a breath. "Your unhappiness isn't about me or our marriage. I may not be a perfect husband, but I'm decent enough. You may not know it, but I regularly think about you and what would make your life good. I'm not sure why you can't see that.

"The depth of your unhappiness, how beleaguered and unconsidered you feel—that's about you. It's not mine to fix."

As Roger stood stunned by what he'd just said, Sharon shot back, blazing with rage.

"I'm so insulted! How dare you?" she said in a tone that in the past would have sent Roger into a tailspin of regret.

Roger paused a moment and said, "If you choose to rest in the feeling of insult, you're going to miss the point."

FINDING A NEW PEACE

Calm. It's often but not always part of those powerful shifts we make. We may be trembling inside, but some steady place inside of us takes over and seems to pull us along.

As with Denise, who, after nine years of believing there was nothing she could do, told her husband, Paul, that his drinking (and the angry tirades that followed) were frightening her and the kids. She said firmly, with not one hint of anger, that the next time he came home drunk she was going to pack them all into the car and go stay with her sister. Even if it was the middle of the night. She said she still loved him and wanted very much to stay married, but she was worn out by the stress and couldn't continue to let the children see him this way. If Paul wanted to keep drinking, so be it. It was his choice.

Or Nadim, who had chronically lied to his wife, Katha, about his spending—shredding receipts, agreeing to take over the bill paying so she wouldn't know that he'd spent nearly $600 for a custom-made iPad cover, $1,200 for a jacket he never wore, telling her he'd be reimbursed for exorbitant lunches that he'd eaten alone.

One day the whole charade felt like too much. He was tired of lying, tired of the distance that lying required him to keep, tired of being out of control. Tired of feeling wretched about how low he had sunk.

That night, after the kids were asleep, he told Katha that he wanted to talk. He handed her a printed stack of credit card statements, the check ledger, and the two credit cards in his wallet. "Full disclosure," he told her, prepared to face whatever came next.

"I went into it having no idea what Katha would do," he said in our session. "Would she want a divorce? Would she ever trust me again? *Whatever happens happens*, I thought. Finally I was telling the truth. Even if she hadn't been as understanding as she was, I would still not have regretted having come clean. It was one of the best nights of my life."

Roger, on the other hand, described his encounter with Sharon as more of an all-time low. The profound sense of calm that he'd initially felt, his quiet resolve—all of that was quickly replaced by out-and-out dread. With what he'd said to Sharon, with how direct and uncompromising he'd been, he was fully convinced that he'd broken the last straw. "It's like the cartoon character who runs off the cliff," he said. "There I was, hanging in thin air, waiting to drop."

It wasn't until days later, when Sharon started to criticize Roger for having parked too far from the curb and had stopped herself in midsentence, that he began to suspect that he'd gotten Sharon's attention, that she'd taken his words to heart. Maybe they would at last be on a healthier track. Maybe their marriage would survive after all. Roger began to feel a lot less angry at Sharon, less afraid to speak up, less afraid of her wrath. She'd become less scary to him, and consequently he behaved in ways that seemed less scary to her. He was then able to see Sharon's hair-trigger reactivity as just that: reactivity, anxiety, and not wrath at all.

When people ask "What's a good move to make when my spouse interrupts? When she brings her computer to bed? When he refuses to talk?," I tell them that a good move is anything that breaks you out of your automatic response pattern and sets you on a healthier course.

It might be no more than a single word or a sentence, spoken out loud or as a reminder to ourselves: *Pause. Be nice. We're about to go down the drain.* It might be a change of expression or a shift in your posture, such as sitting back in your chair when you're having a heated discussion instead of being poised at the edge, as if ready to pounce.

Frequently, the right move can seem like the wrong one: volunteering to do more than we think is fair; speaking up though we may get ourselves into hot water; shutting up when we really, *really* want to mouth off. And what works one time may fall flat the next. Again, it's a matter of *try this* and *try that*, keeping in mind that breaking long-standing patterns can be difficult, slow, disorienting, and even terrifying.

Almost universally, the shift we make allows us to take a step back, to see our partner as separate, to focus on our own feelings, our own point of view, to challenge assumptions that we had mistaken for truths.

The prevailing belief since quite early on in Maggie and Jen's fifteen-year relationship was that Maggie was not a warm and nurturing person. The lack of affection was an issue Jen regularly complained about and Maggie regularly felt powerless to change. Jen had refused to do couples therapy, convinced that the problem was Maggie's to fix. Maggie had grown up with parents who were distant and chilly; she had few memories of being comforted or touched. Jen's characterization of her as a "cold fish" was one Maggie went along with, even though it didn't quite fit her internal sense of who she was.

One day, as she sat snuggled in a blanket with their three-year-old daughter, Eliza, the two of them making goofy animal sounds, Maggie began to question the explanation of why she and Jen weren't as warm and loving as they both said they wanted to be. Deeply aware of her own warm, playful nature, it began to dawn on Maggie that the distance between them wasn't all about her. Yes, she was at times somewhat cool, but Jen was "no bonfire of love and affection herself." Jen was moody and needed a lot of alone time. Often she'd come to bed after Maggie was asleep.

Maggie described it as a moment of personal window washing, as if the windows on the truth were suddenly sparkling clean.

"I was more interested in why I had bought her construction in the first place than I was in convincing her that it was inaccurate. My thought was, the next time Jen complained that our lack of closeness was about me, I'd call her bluff. I'd reach for her. I'd say, 'Okay, what about now?'

"I'm done feeling guilty and ashamed and taking on all the blame. I really would like to be closer to Jen. It remains to be seen if she'd really like to be closer to me."

STOP RUNNING IN CIRCLES

On the bulletin board next to my desk is a cartoon that sums up what I believe about our big-picture struggles. On the right is a breathless hamster running full tilt on his wheel. On the left, a second hamster looks on, contented, sitting perfectly still.

To his frazzled companion he says, "I've had an epiphany!"

Simple, right? If we're tired of running in circles, we can just get off the wheel.

So why don't we do that?

I remember learning in graduate school that when something we do doesn't work, we're likely to do more of it, only louder or more forcefully. I also learned that change is anxiety-provoking. So, miserable or not, we stick with what we know. Both of these points provide, at least, a partial explanation.

My favorite explanation (the one I've learned from experience) is that we run on our hamster wheel because it's there. Because we're already running. Because, unlike our hamster friend, we haven't yet had an epiphany.

Alternatives are everywhere, but in order to see them, to utilize them, we not only have to stop running, we have to be so sick and tired of running that we're willing to step off the wheel and face whatever comes next:

Sharon's several days of bone-chilling silence after Roger confronted her.

Paul's surly insistence that Denise's response to his drinking was over the top.

Jen's steady stream of excuses when Maggie approached

her—*You know I don't like surprises. Your hands are always so clammy. You seem insincere*—until finally Jen could no longer deny her own ambivalence about getting close.

We start by identifying our big-picture issues, calling our problem by its right name. From there we can either continue to run on the wheel of our tedious content, our airtight story lines, our ridiculous rules—or, like hamster number two, we can decide to sit down.

———

Eva and Will had been talking about his affair. Again. It was their impasse, the sticking point in every meaningful conversation they'd had in the two years since Will had had a fling with one of the moms at their son's preschool. Whenever Eva brought up the affair, Will would say, "It's over. Forget it." Always there was some variation of "Why can't we move on?"

On this day, he'd used the phrase "Let sleeping dogs lie," and Eva had quipped that *sleeping* and *lying* was an interesting choice of words.

There they were, once again, stepping onto the wheel, once again about to be locked in their gridlock, with Eva wanting to talk about her uneasiness, her ongoing lack of trust, and Will burned out on discussing it.

Sure, Eva would have loved to move on, but that was easier said than done. There were too many reminders and awkward encounters, too many *here-we-go-again* moments that made her feel sick. Every kids' birthday party. Every school picnic. Having to wonder *Will she be there? Should I just stay home?*

Just a few days earlier Eva had picked up Will's cell phone to find a text message from an unknown number.

"I'm ready! Are you?" it said.

Seeing that had nearly made Eva throw up.

Fortunately, the text had turned out to be from their neighbor, who'd been waiting for Will to come over and help troubleshoot his Wi-Fi.

Still, Eva wanted to talk about it with Will: to tell him how angry and scared she had felt, how she was still on guard. Will, on the other hand, would sooner be boiled in oil.

It's pointless, Eva thought, hearing Will tell her again that he was done talking, that she ought to get over it, that it was over and done. Why bother explaining for the ten billionth time that "getting over it" wasn't the point?

That's when she challenged Will to say something new. "Try it," she said, surprising herself with the suggestion. "Every time we have this conversation, I say the exact same thing and so do you. Come on. I dare you. Say something new."

Will just stared at her blankly, as if nothing new came to mind.

"Say anything," she'd prompted, "except what you always say. Tell me I look nice. Tell me you're scared. Tell me you know that I'm still really hurt and it makes perfect sense."

Will stood there in silence for well over a minute, gulping in a way that looked to Eva as though he were fighting back tears.

"Okay. Talk," he said softly, making it clear that he was ready to listen.

DISCOVERING YOUR OWN WAY TO GET UNSTUCK

Often the solutions we arrive at are simple. They're obvious, ordinary—so ordinary that they can be easily overlooked, easily seen as too simple to make any real difference.

Clients tell me they feel stuck, though I can see they're not. They'll describe a powerful move they made without having recognized that it was powerful at all.

One man whose spouse would declare "This conversation is over!" whenever difficult issues arose abandoned his usual rant about how she "shuts him down" and replied, "Actually, no. I'm not done talking about this."

Another, in a similar situation, paused before chasing after his wife to demand that they talk. *Why is she running?* he wondered. *Why does she find this conversation so threatening?*, realizing in that moment that he'd discovered the very questions he needed to ask *her*.

Breaking out of your gridlocked pattern is not rocket science. The way out—no matter how locked down you are or how long you've been stuck—is to move. It's as simple as that. Sometimes your move will be a big game changer, sometimes it won't. And quite likely, you won't know on the spot. Remember, change happens slowly. You may have to make your move many times (and perhaps in many ways) before being able to tell what impact it's had.

If you were my client and were seeking ways to get yourself unstuck, I might ask, "What's the most frustrating aspect of your repetitive struggle?" Not the content that you revisit

211

(which is certainly frustrating) but the key element in your dynamic that makes you feel trapped or hopeless or off-the-wall nuts. "Which part of your stuckness would you like to see move?"

Maybe it's the way you go bonkers when your spouse claims that you're overreacting, immediately proving his point. Or the way your conflicts hit a dead end, how, no matter what the issue, you feel as if you've driven straight into a brick wall. Maybe there are "off-limits" topics that you'd like to discuss, but the minute you open your mouth your partner bursts into tears. Maybe you're tired of having to back off.

If you're like most of my clients, the most frustrating aspect of your repetitive struggle is that you can't envision a way out.

That's it in a nutshell: we need to discover a way out. We need to create a door in our brick wall so that instead of driving into it, we step through.

The question, of course, is *how?*

Some of our most powerful openings come from the internal shifts we make—a change in the way we conduct ourselves, a challenge to a long-held belief or assumption, a shift in perspective, where we see ourself or our spouse in a new way.

Maybe you realize that your stubbornness or self-righteousness is the key element keeping you stuck. Or you've been keeping a mental ledger, noting your partner's shortcomings and overlooking his strengths, and you now see the importance of changing your ways. Maybe your first move will be to make an unspoken commitment to be more loving and generous or less inclined to dig in. Or you'll vow to calm down when your spouse gets nasty rather than immediately responding in kind. One client decided that at least once a week she would initiate sex, rather than complain about not being able to remember the last time they had gotten it on.

There are times, as well, when we need to step forward to address an issue head-on, by asking a question or stating what we believe to be true:

"I'm concerned that you might have started smoking again. Am I right?"

"When you say 'I can't do this anymore,' are you seriously talking about leaving me or are you just saying that because you're at your wits' end?"

"You may not agree with me that we're overspending, but I feel confident that I'm right."

"I'm done saying 'Okay, fine' just because you're pitching a fit."

Sometimes our statements are more protective than confrontational, designed to steer the relationship out of harm's way. Maybe we call for a time-out or we say, "We can do better" or "Let's have a do-over," or we simply name the destructive pattern that we see happening in the moment:

"We're about to get into name-calling."

"I'm losing my perspective."

"I'm having a hard time not being defensive or mean."

Much like giving a weather report—saying "It's starting to rain" or "It's too icy to drive"—we make an objective, neutral statement about the relationship "climate" so that we can better see what we really need to address.

Then there are moves that add an element of silliness. We can, as one client did, insist that if we're going to keep arguing we have to stand on one foot or speak in a foreign accent. Or, as another proposed, "Let's decide this by thumb wrestling. Best two out of three." One of Patrick's most disarming moves when we're starting to bicker is to reach for my hands and say "Let's dance."

When he does, I recognize how far we have come, despite many false starts and countless dead ends, despite the frustration of trying and failing and trying again.

As I sit with my clients, I keep in mind the courage it takes to persevere, to have a vision for something better, to take the first step toward change, to keep going against what can seem like great odds.

Though I've said that the moves we make are often simple, not for a moment do I think they are easy. We start where we are, and we make whatever move we can. Ready. Not ready. Overwhelmed. Emboldened. Convinced that all hell will break loose if we open our mouth. We try something new because what we've done in the past keeps us stuck in a place that's far worse than our fear of the unknown.

When Roger said that he felt like the cartoon character who had gone over the edge, I thought, *Absolutely! That's just what it's like.* Only somehow we sprout wings. Instead of falling to earth, we discover that we can fly.

The Takeaway:

Hidden in Plain Sight

- At any time, one partner can make a unilateral move. And one move is all that it takes to disrupt the systemic pattern, to introduce change.

- Don't feel bad if the moves you make don't work miracles. Remember: change is a trial-and-error, fall-seven-times-stand-up-eight endeavor.

- As we become stronger, our moves can be bolder.

Part Three

WELCOME TO YOUR STRONGER, MORE LOVING RELATIONSHIP

How to Keep Learning and Growing— Separately and Together

11

360 DEGREES AND SUNNY

The surprising truth about
what makes happy couples happy

You bring your own weather to the picnic.
—GRETCHEN RUBIN

People talk about being happily (or unhappily) married, but what does that mean? When Patrick and I are getting along and feeling close, when we're warm and loving and doing our best, of course we would say that we're happily married. It can seem almost effortless, the way we speak gently and touch lovingly, how our communications go smoothly. Even the bumps aren't all that big of a deal. But there's more to being happily married than knowing how to thrive when life is good. The real challenge for couples is to figure out how to be happily married during the hard times as well.

Back when I was struggling in my marriage, everyone looked happier than Patrick and me. On every street corner, in every café, every couple seemed to be radiating rainbows. It was hard to imagine them arguing about the idiotic nonsense that had us going in circles and equally hard to imagine that we'd ever learn how to stop.

Maybe the happier couples were more compatible from the outset, I thought. Or they were smarter or luckier when choosing their spouse. Maybe their marriages had come with an instruction book. Maybe they were better able to follow instructions.

It turns out that what really makes happy couples happy is something I'd never considered: *they aren't always happy.*

At least not 24/7, jump-for-joy happy.

Happy couples don't always speak calmly or start every argument with a statement of gratitude. They don't feel Fourth-of-July fireworks each and every time they make love, nor do they expect to. Sometimes they exchange heated words or slam doors or roll their eyes in frustration. Sometimes they go to bed angry or one of them sleeps on the couch. Sometimes they look exactly like unhappy couples—at least on the outside.

The difference, I discovered, is what they do on the inside.

I remember the first time I heard Jim say that it's our job to make ourselves happy in our relationship.[1] It was during one of our first case consultations. We were talking about a couple who had taken to eating three meals a day in a restaurant because they couldn't agree about who would cook and clean up, let alone what they would eat. Both of them claimed to be unhappy with the arrangement, blaming their plight on the other's inflexibility.

What does it mean, make ourselves happy? Who can be happy with a spouse who constantly yells at you, belittles you, or refuses to talk? What if he gambles or can't keep a job?

"I don't expect my clients to live in wedded bliss," I conceded to Jim, "but I won't deny that many couples have serious issues to face. How can people be happy when they feel embattled or trapped in a relationship where there's no life and no connection, with no idea how to make anything better?" I asked, obviously revealing my worst fears about the prospects for my own marriage.

"Of course they have serious issues to face. We all have serious issues in our relationships," Jim responded gently. "But, Winifred, remember, nobody is required to stay married. It's a choice that we make. If you, or any of us, is going to stay with our partner, it's our job to figure out how to be happy in whatever way we can, in whatever way that is."

Unless, of course, you can't, I muttered to myself.

The whole idea seemed preposterous. Or perhaps just unimaginable. When I first heard Jim use the phrase "Make yourself happy," Patrick and I had not yet gone to see him. Yes, much had improved in our marriage, but we were at best caught in an eddy, living more like roommates than lovers and now and again living like enemies. Just hearing Jim say the word *happy* made me feel like an outsider looking in. Despite all the truly good things in our marriage, I feared that the bad would win. I believed, at the time, that my happiness was in Patrick's hands. I'd be happy if he hung up his coat, if he threw out his junk mail, if he stopped blaming me for the unhappiness he felt.

I'd never thought about taking the initiative to make myself happier in my marriage. As far as I knew, being happily married wasn't an item one put on a to-do list. I thought happiness was simply a by-product of an already good marriage, like interest compounding on a sizable bank account. Happiness was the intangible sweetness that wafted through the lives of successful couples like the smell of chocolate chip cookies fresh from the oven. Happiness belonged to those lucky match-made-in-heaven couples who didn't waste their time bickering or digging in their heels. It was for people who knew how to cooperate and were willing to compromise. People unlike Patrick and me.

When I talk to couples about finding ways to make themselves happy in their relationship, most are as surprised as I was to hear that it's their job at all. "So what's my partner's job?" they ask, failing to consider that their partner might be hard at work trying to figure how to live happily with them.

When a prevailing belief in our culture is that people should either leave a relationship that doesn't make them happy or pressure their partner to improve his or her performance, no wonder so few of us have any idea where to begin. The notion that we might find ways to live happily under less-than-ideal circumstances can seem insulting or laughable or even, in some cases, impossible.

CAN YOU MAKE YOURSELF HAPPY?

To hear Richard tell it, you'd think he'd been the victim of some terrible ruse. "It was just like those stories you hear about people getting their luggage mixed up at the airport and going home with a suitcase that looks just like theirs—except, of course, for what's inside." Richard was married to a woman who would spend days without speaking to him after a fight. In the months before I first saw them, the ratio between "silent treatment" and "normal life" had been approaching three to one, and Richard was fit to be tied.

In their first years together, Lena had been soft-spoken and kind, though a bit on the shy side. Richard loved her sense of humor, her sharp eye for detail, her brilliant mind. They'd laughed together; they'd read books together; they'd fallen in love. Life was good, and then . . . something went wrong. Richard said things had taken a downturn soon after their son, Max, was born. Short on sleep and overtaxed, Lena became irritable, critical, easily hurt. Lena said that she was the very same person she'd been all along but it was Richard who wanted her to be someone she's not. According to Lena, Richard had changed, asking for—no, *demanding*—attention when, obviously, she had little to give.

Either way, Richard was convinced that the warmhearted woman he'd married had been spirited away and an icy facsimile had been left in her place.

The story of Lena's childhood read like a Dickens novel, with dreadful poverty and far too many mouths to feed. Lena's father, a drunk and womanizer, had left the family scrabbling to make ends meet and had ultimately gone missing on her twelfth birthday, never to be seen or heard from again. Any of Richard's actions that even hinted at thoughtlessness— forgetting to lock a door, mismanaging the checkbook, even things as innocent as his returning from a business trip with a cold that he passed on to Max—ignited Lena's fury and prompted retreat as the traumatic pain of her childhood overtook her once more.

For Richard, this was devastating, as he'd been an only child of severely depressed parents and had spent countless hours in his room, wishing for company, longing for love, wondering what he might do to make his parents cheer up. When Lena withdrew, Richard, too, was thrust back to his childhood struggles, doing what he had learned to do as a child: blaming himself, often begging for a forgiveness that, given Lena's history, would not be forthcoming.

"Maybe we're just wrong for each other," Richard posited one day, as the perfect fit of his individual issues and Lena's became painfully clear. This most troublesome aspect of linking is what Jim liked to call a couple's match-made-in-hell place, where the unique interlock of both partners' issues offers no obvious escape from their dilemmas.

Picture a saver who marries a spender or someone who is easily wounded who chooses a partner who frequently points out her flaws or the world-renowned pastry chef whose wife is perpetually dieting and doesn't like sweets. In a seemingly unfortunate, mysterious way, we choose a partner who will put us up against the issues we most need to address—a need for validation or acceptance, a need for control—and then get in our way as we try to address them. Not out of malice and not to intentionally frustrate us, but simply because they are who they are.

As much as we long for our spouse to help resolve our dilemma—to get out of our way, to live life as we prefer—we will grow stronger (clearer, steadier) by finding a way out all on our own. It's up to us to grow, surrender, or tear out our hair. It's up to us to figure out how to be happy with the partner we picked.

HAPPINESS IS OPTIONAL

None of us *needs* to be happy in order to survive. In fact, research has shown that our brain's natural tendency is to be drawn to what's wrong: to scan our environment for potential threats to our survival, not to help us seek ways to experience greater pleasure. Vigilance and caution are states that are hardwired; peace and happiness are states we must learn.[2] Seen in this light, happiness is a quality-of-life issue; it's something we strive to attain because it enriches our life and brings us deeper fulfillment. Even so, it is something we can literally live without.

Like all happiness, being happy in our relationship is something we choose, much like the choice we have either to be driven crazy by things that our partner does or to figure out ways to keep ourselves sane. But learning to tolerate the imperfect world of dawdling and clutter, flaring tempers and blame is one thing; making oneself happy in the face of these things is another entirely.

As one client asked, "How can you be happy and unhappy at the same time?"

Many people think that in order to be happy they'll have to talk themselves into liking what they hate. They use phrases such as "Suck it up," "Grin and bear it," and "Make do." Many people fear that the pursuit of their own happiness will give their partner carte blanche to act like an ass. "How's that different from being a doormat?" some ask as they imagine themselves suffering in silence while their partner gets off scot free.

But making yourself happy isn't about being a martyr, gnashing your teeth in grim determination, or being silent about issues that need to be addressed; nor is it about hardening your heart with indifference while claiming to be "at peace." One client proudly announced that she "no longer cared" about the eighteen-hour workdays her partner regularly put in. "I'm totally fine with it," she insisted, her voice so unfeeling that she seemed in a trance.

Seeking happiness in the face of our difficulties requires that we in fact do care a great deal—about ourselves, our partner, and our life together. It means making a choice to be as happy as possible in whatever way we can, even though there are some things we're not happy about in the least. I'd be lying if I said I feel happy each time I find tea leaves all over the counter or when Patrick insists I speed up when there's no-where to go or interrupts me to point out the ways he thinks I'm wrong. Fortunately, being happily married isn't the same as living happily ever after.

One day, after a particularly painful few days of estrangement, Richard came into my office and threw up his hands. "I finally get it. It's my move," he said, hands above his head as if being held at gunpoint. Faced with the choice either to be driven to despair by Lena's icy withdrawal or to figure out ways to deal with his distress, he was ready to take steps toward the latter.

Therapy had made things better, he said, but not better enough.

He and Lena had recognized by this point that much of their conflict was fueled by their pasts. Seeing only the other's mis-steps and reactions had re-created the helplessness they'd felt as children, making everything worse. As they began to focus on themselves instead, their fights became fewer and their re-pairs became easier. Both came to recognize that their actions could either fuel or subdue a coming firestorm. Both accepted that the painful feelings inside them were theirs to resolve.

More and more, Lena would apologize for overreacting. More and more, rather than fleeing, she'd come back to the table willing to work things out. In time, Richard recognized that ingratiating himself to Lena did more harm than good. All his pleading and apologizing riled her to no end and served only to "prove" him to be shallow—and sniveling, to boot; no better, Lena said, than the low-life father she'd despised all her life.

Most painful of all was how his habit of groveling left Richard feeling cheapened and small, as if he'd sold himself out for a scrap of affection. Tiptoeing around Lena's reactivity, he concluded, was as bad for their marriage as it was for him.

Yet despite their hard work and forward movement, there were still times that Lena withdrew into silence. Not very often nor for very long, but it happened nonetheless. For Richard, even once in a blue moon was too frequent, as almost immediately his feelings of isolation became intolerable. Flooded with anxiety, he'd set off on a tirade, shouting a string of what Lena referred to as his *un-thises* and *un-thats*: unacceptable . . . untenable . . . unreasonable . . . unwarranted—which only drove Lena into further retreat.

"When we first came to see you, I honestly expected that you'd turn to Lena and say, 'This has got to stop!' And really, don't laugh," Richard said, "I actually thought that just your saying it would make her comply! Apparently I need to devise a plan B."

Though it was quite challenging at first, Richard found ways to meet the chilly days with greater composure. "I'm an adult now," he'd remind himself when his old childhood loneliness threatened to drown him. "I have a really good life," he'd say, bolstering himself with his mostly believable pep talk.

Some days he'd take Max and go to the park, where they'd laugh and have fun, rather than stay home and wait for Lena to thaw, as he'd done for years. Or he'd go for long walks with the dog or catch up on his reading. Once in a while he'd do what I'd done: go out on his porch and take some deep breaths or look at the sky. Sometimes he'd talk to Lena as if everything were "normal," asking if she'd like a sandwich or reading something of interest aloud from the newspaper. Now and again she'd lighten up and respond. To his relief, Richard learned not to get hooked by Lena's scowl or her dramatically averted gaze when she was too dug in to budge. And he stopped apologizing over and over, recognizing that Lena's need to withdraw was her issue, not his. He finally understood that he didn't deserve exile no matter what he had done. Sometimes he had glimmers of compassion for both Lena and himself. Life had been much better, he said, once he'd stopped needing Lena to warm up any faster than she did.

A NEW WAY TO LOOK AT HAPPINESS

Making ourselves happy is about taking full responsibility for the experiences we have in our relationship. Despite challenges, beyond circumstances, no matter how different we are from our spouse. If we aren't going to leave, it's our job to figure out how to not just survive but thrive.

Quite often, making ourselves happy comes back to what Einstein said about differences, that we must not only learn to tolerate our differences but welcome them, to appreciate the richness and true intelligence (and growth) they offer us.

Many clients speak of having adopted a more accepting attitude toward their differences. Things that once seemed intolerable have been downgraded to an annoyance. And eventually annoyance is downgraded to "Oh, well." I hear clients say things such as:

"It stopped mattering so much."

"Over time I got used to it."

"I realized it's just not worth fighting about."

"Life is too short."

They speak about flexibility, openness, and coming to peace—often quite pleased with how they found ways to get around what once had seemed like an irresolvable impasse.

When I asked Patrick what he thought he'd done to be happier in our marriage, he said that he'd decided to pay attention to the things he loves about me: the enthusiasm I bring to having a healthier marriage, the fact that I'm eager and able to rewire a lamp, that when he's having a difficult day I'm likely to bring him a cup of tea or give him a neck rub or put flowers on his desk. Better to focus on those things, he said, than to stew about how many times I turn around and go back into the house to get whatever thing I forgot before I finally get out the door. Better than another futile attempt to have me be more like him.

A friend recently said that he had become much happier in his marriage after raising the standards for his own behavior and lowering the expectations he had of his wife. "You know, Colleen hasn't gotten any easier," he said. "The difference is that I now act like a grown-up regardless of what she does." When I asked why that made him happier, he said that finally he was being the kind of husband he wanted his sons to become.

One long-married client made herself happy by reclaiming parts of herself that she'd given up. She started wearing sparkly scarves, listening to opera while she cooked, keeping fresh flowers on her dresser—all things her husband found to be frivolous. "The better I feel about myself, my own life, the way I move through the world, the less cranky I am about having married a man who may well have been happy being a monk. It's much easier to love and appreciate him when I don't let him cramp my style."

Another client equated learning to live with his wife's constant flurry of activity to how people adjust to living near train tracks. "Eventually it becomes background noise," he said as he came to live peacefully within himself—a shift he'd never dreamed he'd accomplish. "What other options did I have?" he asked with a shrug, echoing the sentiments many of us share.

Many clients have said that focusing on choice plays a powerful role in how they make themselves happy:

"I look around at other people's marriages, other people's husbands, and I realize that I wouldn't want to trade places with any of them. I'd rather be dealing with our problems than dealing with theirs."

"I remind myself that I knew what I was getting myself into, choosing someone who reads all the time. It's one of the things that makes Jackie an interesting (and happy) person. Even though I end up spending more time alone than I'd like, in all honesty, I wouldn't want her to be someone else."

"I used to fantasize that somewhere out there is the perfect person for me. I used to feel sorry for myself, thinking *Irene is not that person*. I eventually realized that there is no perfect person. Everyone is going to have flaws. Accepting this, accepting Irene, is a huge relief."

"When Mike is driving me nuts, I ask myself if I want to stay or leave. When my answer is that I want to stay, I stop blaming him for being the person I picked."

Figuring out how to be happy can be nearly impossible when couples feel as if they have no choice. Some of the most unhappily married people I've met are those who are staying together because they feel they must. In some cases their religion dictates that they cannot divorce. Or they have an ill or at-risk child and fear the consequences of dismantling the family. Others have been told that it will devastate their partner/mother/bridge club, so they stay married, resigned to run out the clock on what feels like a life sentence.

A friend of mine who was married to a man who went full-on bonkers over every penny she spent dreamed that she'd been granted one wish. Without hesitation—*poof!*—she turned her husband into a topiary. Another admitted to having visions of his husband taking a job in Siberia. Dreading all that divorce would entail, I used to fantasize that Patrick would be abducted by aliens. Many people I know have had far darker fantasies than these.

Clients have come in confessing that they hate their spouse, that over time the conditions of their marriage had deteriorated to the point that just looking at their partner set their teeth on edge. Most said they feel trapped, that they see no escape from their struggles, that they have little or no choice about how things go in their marriage—as if they were in prison and their spouse held the key.

Back when I was contemplating Patrick's abduction by aliens, I, too, felt trapped. All I could see were the small-picture details: too many arguments that never went anywhere, frustrating interactions that left me feeling worn out and hopeless. I had no idea what was keeping us stuck—and I knew even less about the possibilities of making myself happy.

When Jim said that if we want to be happily married it's up to us, he was essentially saying "Here are the keys." His message, that we can stay or we can leave, made it clear that if we choose to stay we're wasting our time having buyer's remorse.

Which brings us to Richard and his quest to be happier in his marriage to Lena.

Once he was no longer afraid of Lena's sharp tongue or frosty glare and no longer hobbled by the heart-wrenching loneliness he'd felt during her silences, Richard began to feel free—freer, perhaps, than ever before. Free in a way that he felt able to do anything, go anywhere, face everything—able to move himself a full 360 degrees without being worried about what might constrict his movement or what he might bump into. At times, he felt euphoric—invincible, in fact—having found for the first time in his life that he could hold himself steady. His mood, the feelings inside him, his own sense of himself as a husband, as a man, those were inviolable, indelible: his alone, no matter what Lena did.

That was what made all the difference, he said. No longer being afraid. Holding his head up. Feeling solid and whole. That, he said, was happiness enough.

THE AGONY AND THE ECSTASY

When all is said and done, most of us arrive at a place of acceptance. Rather than continuing to dwell on our inevitable frustrations, we settle down and go about the business of discovering how best to live with our partner—frustrations and all. We find ways to be more considerate and compassionate (with our spouse and ourselves) and less attached to having things be as we prefer. We focus on our own growth and development, challenging ourselves to speak up, to take risks, to behave in ways that make us feel good about ourselves. We shift our attention to the things we enjoy and find ways to calm down and maintain perspective about the things we dislike.

A few years ago, I worked with a young, newly married couple who came to see me because the woman, Camille, was deeply worried that their marriage had taken a wrong turn. Marriage wasn't quite what she had expected, Camille said, and with their first anniversary coming in a matter of weeks, she worried they might not make it through year number two.

When I asked "What's the trouble?" Camille said she'd begun to find some of Elliot's behaviors to be downright annoying. The way he stuffed his clean, unfolded laundry into the dresser, how he said "Hmmm" out loud while reading the paper, how he picked at his nails. Sometimes he ate food off his plate with one hand while holding his fork in the other. Sometimes he grumbled when she asked him for help. Her irritation, she feared, was the first sign that the honeymoon was over and they were on the way down.

"Lately," she admitted with lowered voice, "there are things about Elliot I find hard to adore."

Leaving no time for me to comment, she leaned forward and grabbed hold of my arm. "Are you and your husband still ecstatically happy?" she asked. "You know . . . I mean . . . are you madly in love?"

Ecstatically happy? Madly in love?

Starry-eyed as I'd been when I was her age, even I hadn't dreamed that having a good marriage would require that I feel perpetually ecstatic or head over heels. My mind quickly went to how that very morning I'd tripped over the bathroom scale that Patrick had left sticking out from under the counter, quite likely breaking my toe. In no way had that left me feeling ecstatic. I thought of the misconceptions I'd had as a newlywed about marriage and love and recognized the desperation that comes with thinking that something is terribly wrong, when in fact, nothing is.

My first impulse was to blurt out, "You've got to be kidding!," but Camille was far too tender for that, and she'd been utterly serious. For her, no longer adoring everything about Elliot had come to signify the beginning of the end.

The two of them waited, wide-eyed, as I gathered my thoughts, Camille tightly gripping my arm as if I were a life raft. Elliot, in the meantime, had gone white as a sheet. He'd been as surprised as I by Camille's outlandish ideas, nervously laughing at first and then barely taking a breath. Understandably, he was worried that the future of his marriage hinged upon whether or not Patrick and I still lived in a state of unceasing bliss.

I placed a steadying hand on top of Camille's, quickly running through options about how best to respond. I thought of how helpful it would have been to have learned, early on in my marriage, that not every problem can be solved and not every irritant can be negotiated away, that a good marriage is a mixture of delight and disgruntlement, that unhappiness comes from expecting it to be otherwise.

The bar she'd set was impossibly high. But Camille wasn't the first person to have unrealistic notions about married life. When marriage turns out to be more difficult than they'd originally imagined, when couples realize they've stopped feeling "madly in love," many fear that their marriage is disintegrating or that they've picked the wrong spouse.

Had Camille asked me this question before Patrick and I had done our intensive with Jim, my response would have been guarded and vague. Until I'd made peace with the never-to-end nuisance of jackets on doorknobs and shoes underfoot—or things even harder, such as the thankfully rare but still possible rerun of our painful competition over who had wronged whom—I'd have been hiding my own hurt and disappointment that I was yet to work through.

I looked at Camille, finally ready to speak. "My husband and I have been together for what feels like a lifetime," I said. "We were young when we met, and it took many years to grow up. It hasn't been easy, but marriage isn't easy for any of us. With all we've been through together, I love him dearly—but neither of us is ecstatic. And thank goodness, we don't have to be," I added, at which point Camille took a deep breath and softened her grip.

"Forty years of nonstop ecstasy is a lot to ask. Marriage is not about living in bliss, though we've certainly been led to think it should be. Happiness comes from learning how to live well with what's hard to adore. In a good marriage, we strive to love each other in spite of our annoyances and shortcomings. We open our hearts to someone who is imperfect. That includes people who scowl or chew loudly or don't fold their wash.

"You know what?" I said, feeling deeply grateful to be able to say this and mean it. "I'll take being dear, loving friends with someone who loves me as I am over feeling ecstatic any day."

The Takeaway:
360 Degrees and Sunny

- Making ourselves happy is about taking full responsibility for the experience that we have in our relationship. It's about making peace with the things we cannot change.

- We can stay with our partner, or we can leave. If we stay, we might as well figure out how to have a good and satisfying life with that person.

- One of the keys to being happy in your marriage is to live in a way that makes you feel whole and alive.

12

IT TAKES ONE TO TANGO

A pep talk for your journey

If not now, when?
—HILLEL

"What if every morning your husband poked you in the eye with a sharp stick? What would you do then?"

Each time we met, my client Nigel asked that very question or some variation of it, hoping to make a case for why he shouldn't have to deal with his wife's volcanic temper and how my basic theory about marriage is essentially crap.

"What if he stamped on your foot? Spat in your eye? Screamed in your ear? What if you asked him to stop and he didn't?

"Would your philosophy of marriage still hold?"

Every week we went through this series of what-ifs, and every week I stood firm. "Nigel," I said, "you can choose to leave Gloria, or you can stay with her. If you stay, you're left

238

with only two options: you can figure out what to do with your-self in the face of your challenges, or you can let yourself be driven totally nuts."

Nigel was holding out for the third option that he will never be offered: the option that mandates Gloria to change.

I told him what I tell every one of my clients and what I've said in this book: change in a marriage is created unilaterally, not by agreement and never by threat. Change comes about when one person makes a commitment to change him- or her-self. Trying to change the other person is a complete waste of time.

Nigel threw up his arms in a dramatic gesture of innocence, insisting, as always, that he had nothing to change. "Gloria's be-havior is simply not *normal*," he said, citing a recent incident when Gloria had locked him out of the house after his "quick run to the dry cleaners" had turned into an afternoon out on his friend's sailboat. Gloria had been on a rant since early that morning, and though Nigel's escape had been sorely lacking in backbone, I could certainly see why he had chosen to duck out.

Nigel tried once again to punch holes in my theory, restating that everything would be fine if the things that were "broken" in Gloria would somehow get "fixed."

"Come on," he said. "If your husband told you that every day he prays for your death, would you really think that it's your job to figure out what to do with yourself?"

Then he asked me a question he'd never asked me before, not in all our months of work together. "What makes you so sure?" he probed.

"Because this is how I turned around my own marriage," I said. "By changing myself."

DO IT YOURSELF

If I had been Nigel's therapist decades ago, I wouldn't have known to advise him to save his marriage by changing himself. Back then I thought—as most therapists still do—that it takes two people to right a foundering marriage. I believed the conventional wisdom about two-way streets and meeting each other halfway, each person doing fifty percent. Of course marital change requires a shared willingness to grow. What could one partner possibly do on his or her own?

I might have thought, as I heard Nigel's saga, *Yes, Nigel is right. Gloria is indeed a handful.* I might have thought that his situation was hopeless, or I might have suggested that Gloria seek therapy on her own. And I might well have believed that, even then, in being married to Gloria, Nigel would be in for a rough ride.

And with that I would have let both of them down.

This is one of the key problems with the "it takes two" approach: both partners end up in a holding pattern, waiting for the other to make the first move toward change. If change requires two people—each doing his or her part—what would have happened to Patrick and me? And what hope would there be for the countless number of couples I work with, when one spouse is at her wits' end and the other has little or no motivation or believes things are perfectly fine as they are? Or in a marriage like Nigel's, when one partner is a short-fused firecracker and the other is convinced he has nothing to change?

In an ideal world—the world in which two people are willing to tango—both spouses have the desire and ability to approach their differences with a collaborative spirit. They're able to roll up their sleeves under pressure and be patient and calm and come to fair and satisfying agreements. Couples like those don't show up in my office. And I guarantee that my colleagues would say the same goes for them.

Most couples come in with their long list of complaints, convinced, the way I was, that their happiness—in fact, the very future of their marriage—is contingent on their partner shortening that list.

And when that doesn't happen, when they're unable to get each other's buy-in—when one spouse is unable to convince the other to agree to the change they desire—most assume that they've reached a dead end. Some spend years arguing, or they give up and settle for a less-than-satisfying marriage. Some think their only option is to get a divorce.

The alternative, of course, is to stop waiting for your spouse to join in the effort and to get to work on the part that's about you, despite your concerns that it's not fair, that you're not the only person with issues, or that "going it alone" lets your spouse off the hook.

Clients like Nigel have said that I'm asking too much. My do-it-yourself strategy may be just the ticket for others, they say, but not for them. They believe that their particular marital hardship is exceptional, that the struggle in their relationship exceeds the maximum daily limit for unhappiness or unreason-ableness or marital misery. "Certainly my partner should have to change *this*!" they argue, citing instances of thrown coffee mugs, curse words, and children left overtime at day care. The implied message: given their partner's outrageous behaviors, they shouldn't have to confront anything in themselves.

It's true, I'm asking a lot. I'm asking you to design and imple-ment your own action plan, manage your emotional reactivity, even—especially—when your spouse is doing his best to get under your skin. I'm suggesting that you set a high bar for your-self and step outside your comfort zone, with no guarantee as to what will come next.

I'll be the first to admit that changing ourselves is hard work. It was much harder than I had initially expected. Fortunately, though, it was also much more rewarding. Shifting the focus to my role in our dynamic—paying more attention to my actions and reactions and less attention to the ways Patrick sent me over the edge—gave me a sense of control and direction that made all the hard work well worth the effort.

But for me, as for most of my clients, choosing to be the lone agent for change was the last resort. It felt like the path of least resistance, a path that, at the time, looked a lot like giving up. For years, I'd hoped that something—a therapist, a book, a magic wand—would turn Patrick into a person who was easier to live with. All my pushing and prodding hadn't changed anything, nor had our first attempts at therapy. And unfortunately, there was no magic wand. I was going to have to change my marriage singlehandedly, or I was going to have to leave.

Yes, my solo approach was arduous and frustrating and quite lonely at times. And given the challenges, I was often convinced that I would fail. What I didn't know at the outset—in fact, the part I got wrong—was that taking matters into my own hands was anything but an act of giving up. Giving up is when you hold yourself back because your partner is holding himself back, because he's fearful or proud or resistant to change, or because she's run out of hope and is simply hunkering down. Giving up is when you put the brakes on your longing for a healthier, more vital relationship because conventional wisdom says one person shouldn't have to do "more." Once I got past my own issues about fairness and stopped blaming Patrick for the state we were in, I recognized the payoff that comes from taking charge. Signing on as the architect and carpenter in my own marriage remodel was empowering beyond anything I had imagined.

Hallelujah! Finally I wasn't waiting for Patrick to leap up and shout, "Let's change our marriage. I'm ready to go!" Or better still, "Let's start with my picking up all the stuff I've left everywhere, and we'll take it from there." Once I took charge, I was no longer dependent on Patrick's nod of approval. I no longer needed him to hold my hand each step of the way. I was prepared to throw all caution to the wind if that's what it would take to rescue my marriage, and he could join me in that—or not.

Being able to stand on your own is the mark of a powerful

person. Powerful people go out on a limb and have the gumption to stay there. They're able to hold a necessary position, no matter how anxious or isolated or foolhardy they might feel. They don't sit around longing for change or asking permission or waiting for their spouse to give them a round of applause. They keep their own light shining—and wouldn't be caught dead whining about having to go more than halfway.

Taking the lead may not be your first-choice solution. It may not be the strategy you assumed you would need. It may seem like too hard or uncharted a road to travel. You may think you're not adventurous or persistent or optimistic enough to be the front-runner for change. You may think your marriage (or your partner) is too far gone.

If you were sitting with me in my office voicing those thoughts, what I would say is "Give it a go. None of us has tried everything, though we may think we have." I'd ask you to suspend your concerns about what's possible and impossible and to find the strong, hopeful place in yourself that has been longing for change. I'd ask you to imagine that you have everything you need to head out on your journey and to trust that you'll gain strength and wisdom with every step you take.

Go on, pick one place to begin. Make one small change. Take one leap of faith, and see where you land. I've done it myself, as have many hundreds of couples I've worked with, most of us hesitant at first and then glad that we leapt.

I know what it's like to yearn to stretch out, spread your wings, know yourself, use your voice, feel an irresistible pull to reclaim the long-set-aside parts of yourself that are too valuable to forsake. I stood where you're standing now on the night I came home from that first workshop with Ellyn, emboldened by her message to risk, to go against my self-preservation instinct in order to grow, having no idea whatsoever where that would lead. All I knew was that I wanted more. I wasn't willing to settle for a mediocre or even an okay marriage. I was convinced we could create a marriage that was sane and rewarding, a marriage that would not only last but serve as a source of great joy and self-discovery. And I knew that, terrifying as it was, in order to do that, the first step would have to be mine.

EMBRACING WHAT IS REAL

It's Sunday afternoon at 1:45, and, to my amazement, I'm ready to walk. I've already put on my sneakers and left my hat by the door, with fifteen minutes to spare. I've worked for years to come as close to being on time as I possibly can. My goal is to avoid sending Patrick into a tailspin while not feeling oppressively rushed myself. Today I'm ready ahead of schedule. This may be a first.

When you're someone like me, *ready* can be undone in the blink of an eye. There's always one more phone call to make or email to answer, one more plant on the porch in need of a drink. From there, *ready* will slip to *almost ready*, and before you know it, it's become *not ready at all*.

When you're someone like Patrick, each task your spouse

adds before she gets out the door will push you one minute closer to going over your edge.

We know this about each other: my never-ending to-do list, my overoptimistic assessment of how long something will take, his pressing need not to waste time that grows even more pressing the longer I make him wait. We know that trying to get our way by wearing each other down or insisting that the other live life as we do exacts too high a price. We know that given our history, a difference in preferences can become a battle of wills.

But battles like this are no longer worth fighting. As Jim clearly said, every couple will have their intrinsic dilemma that will never resolve. This just happens to be ours.

I think of our Sunday walk as a weekly snapshot of our marriage—a measure of how well we handle ourselves when our most trying differences put us to the test. At this point in our marriage, we're able to meet our differences (mostly) with grace. We're able to laugh and even commiserate about the challenges we present to each other by being who we are. We're able to consider each other's concerns without fearing we'll lose ourselves in the process or end up giving too much. And we can change long-standing patterns just to be kind. I can even be ready for our walk with time on my hands.

If I were to line up every mental snapshot I've taken of Patrick and me over the years, I would see our progression up the developmental ladder. I'd see us as young newlyweds in the early stages of marriage, headstrong and reactive and emotionally joined at the hip. I would see how my learning to calm down and unhook before one or both of us exploded was a needed first step. I would see the day I discovered that when I'm running late I can just say "I'm sorry," instead of criticizing Patrick for being obsessed with time. I would see myself learning when to be quiet and when to speak up, how not to throw gasoline on the fire when Patrick was agitated, how to suggest, once we were out the door, that he might want to find a way to enjoy the walk. I would see the years when our marriage began to feel more like two *I*s than a *we* and that, to my delight, we came full circle, to a deeper, more loving connection than we'd had at the start.

At first it was just me changing myself, looking at my contribution to our difficulties, owning up to the ways my behavior would drive anyone crazy, and seeing how I allowed Patrick to drive me crazy in turn. I had no guarantee that Patrick would do the same. But eventually I was no longer the only one of us changing. Building our marriage became a two-person job.

As we made our way up the developmental ladder, each stage followed the next almost without notice. "Oh, here we are," I would say, recognizing that, at some point, we'd taken another step up. Not so when I realized we'd reached Stage Five, the stage at the top.

As we often do on Saturday nights, Patrick and I had picked out a movie we wanted to watch. I'd gone upstairs to write while he was finishing the dishes, and, no surprise, I lost track of the time. Instead of impatiently calling "When will you be ready?" he came upstairs to my office and put his hand on my arm. "Just let me know if you need extra time. There's no need to rush," he said. "I'm fine either way."

"I'm ready now," I said, stopping my work. "But how about I bank those extra minutes you offered? Chances are that I'll need them tomorrow when I'm running late for our walk."

We had arrived at Stage Five, the stage Pete and Ellyn called *Synergy*. Couples who've worked their way to this final developmental stage are no longer seeking an ideal marriage or mate. They're able to accept imperfections in themselves and their partner and can embrace what is real. This stage allows for a deeper, more intimate connection, as couples know that they're loved as they are, that they no longer need to hide the potentially "unacceptable" parts of themselves the way they did early on. At this point in a couple's development their relationship has an energy of its own that will enliven and enrich the lives of both partners.

I realized that night, as Patrick offered more time and I had declined, the ground of our relationship had shifted from "me versus you" to "We're in this together." Like many of my clients, Patrick and I had struggled to find a balance between advocating for what we wanted for ourselves and supporting the wants and needs of the other person, too often confusing generosity with giving up or giving in. Now it feels good to be kind and to offer support. I like being able to say yes when I can, and when I say no, there's no price to pay. True generosity can come only from a position of strength: from being full enough inside that when we give to each other, we have plenty left for ourselves.

It's been nearly thirty-nine years since the guy in the pickup truck warned us to quit while we were ahead. Patrick and I are both glad we ignored his advice. Despite rough times and discouragement, immaturity and stubbornness, inadequate skills and unrealistic expectations, we did what we needed to do— what I in fact knew in the first ninety minutes of my first training with Ellyn to be our best and last hope: we grew up.

That's the beauty of this work: it helps us grow up. As we learn to stand on our own feet, we grow more sure of ourselves and clearer about our path. No longer needing a guarantee of safety, we are free to take risks. No longer needing our partner to stand by us at all times, we are able to step forward, come what may. With this ability, the surprising result is that we are then able to move closer to each other, be more open, more vulnerable, risk a far greater tenderness than would have been otherwise possible.

One person must take the first step. Why not let that person be you?

ACKNOWLEDGMENTS

Though a journey of a thousand miles may well begin with the first step, when writing a book, a thousand miles barely gets you through your rambling, messy first draft. It's the next thousand miles, and the many thousands after, that shows what you're really made of and, more important, who your friends are, who believes in you, and who's willing to keep believing in you when you can't imagine taking another step.

It is with deepest gratitude and appreciation that I give thanks to all those who supported me on my journey.

I want to begin by thanking my clients. It is because of you and for you that I have written this book. Every day, I am inspired by your courage and resilience, your willingness to challenge yourself (and me). This book is your story as much as it is mine.

Not one word of this book would have been written without the women in my writers' group—Gail Shaffarman, whose call to action brought us together, Pat Kunstenaar, Joyce Scott, Jan Sells, Victoria Werhan—who tirelessly followed this book through its many incarnations. I cannot thank you enough.

ACKNOWLEDGMENTS

The same goes for my dear friends and family who have celebrated every milestone and consoled every setback. Your many years of loving support and enthusiasm were the wind in my sails.

Special thanks to Clare Langley-Hawthorne for her wise perspective that book writing is a war of attrition, and for our pact to meet every hurdle with determination and a good laugh. And to my devoted friend Michael Radkowsky (my personal "comma-czar"), who along with Pat Kunstenaar and my husband, Patrick, read every word of this manuscript more times than any sane person should have to, and did so with immeasurable generosity and joy. This is, unquestionably, the true meaning of love.

I am forever indebted to my agent, Betsy Amster, who believed in this book even when it was a tangled thicket in need of a good pruning. No words can adequately express how grateful I am for your unflagging support, your strong advocacy, and your impeccable guidance. Every author should be as fortunate as I am.

Great thanks, as well, to my editor and friend, Leigh Ann Hirschman, who taught me the value of a good outline and helped me write in a straight line instead of in circles. My only regret in finishing this book is that I will have fewer opportunities to laugh with you on the phone about writing and marriage and the wild ride both entail. I may need to write another book just to indulge in that pleasure again.

To the many people at Touchstone who have had a hand in this project—I thank each and every one of you, seen and unseen. Special thanks to Michelle Howry for seeing the potential in this book and making it happen; my editor, Lauren Spiegel, whose warmth and no-nonsense good judgment guided me every step of the way; Jessie Chasan-Taber, a one woman administrative miracle who kept track of a never-ending succession of details, and kept me on track with all of them; and Susan Moldow, who stepped in when I needed her most. Thanks, as well, to my publicist, Shida Carr, who has an amazing way of getting people to say yes, and to Meredeth Vilarello for sending my book, far and wide, into the world. From the cover to the last page, you made good on the promise that this book would be a satisfying and wholly collaborative effort.

I consider myself to be extraordinarily blessed by the wisdom and integrity of the teachers who have guided me. I owe my successes to your knowledge and generosity and the high bar you have set personally and as clinicians. Thank you to Ellyn Bader and Pete Pearson for your many years of thoughtful guidance, your fierce commitment to the field of couples therapy, and your kind permission to pass on the value of your work to my readers. Thank you, as well, to Noel Larson and Jim Maddock for opening your hearts and your home to those of us fortunate enough to have studied with you. All of your voices come through me as I work.

And finally, I want to thank my husband, Patrick, without whom this book would (quite literally) not exist. Picture an entire page of thank-yous, single spaced. You have been, at once, a worthy opponent and loving companion. I chose you forty-two years ago and, challenging as our hardest times were, I would choose you again in a heartbeat.

TYPICAL AND NORMAL WAYS PEOPLE AVOID DIFFERENTIATION

I blame my partner, see him or her as the problem.

I talk to my friends instead of my partner.

I tell myself my partner could not handle my real feelings.

I make an attempt . . . then give up, thinking I've tried everything.

I get very upset . . . flooded with everything that's ever been wrong.

I try to forget it . . . keep smiling.

I go numb, hold it in, hope to avoid any conflict.

I blurt it out . . . have a nasty fight.

I minimize or deny my own shortcomings to avoid feeling wrong or one-down.

I tell myself my partner will never change . . . what's the use?

I distract myself . . . focus on something else.

I don't feel much . . . nothing really bothers me.

I change the subject.

I get angry at someone or something else.

I get busy . . . I work harder . . . there's so much to do.

I work on letting go and practicing "non-attachment" rather than acknowledging a problem or taking a stand.

I tell myself I'll get even . . . eventually.

I think of the suffering of saints and others . . . life is *dukkha*.

I try not to let my partner see how bothered I really am.

I drop hints, verbally or through my body language.

I use drugs and/or alcohol to avoid dealing with my discomfort.

I threaten to leave or console myself with these thoughts.

NOTES

2. WHY MARRIAGE CAN BE SO HARD

1 Ellyn Bader and Peter T. Pearson, *In Quest of the Mythical Mate: A Developmental Approach to Diagnosis and Treatment in Couples Therapy* (Florence, KY: Brunner/Mazel, 1988).

2 Margaret Mahler, *The Psychological Birth of the Human Infant: Symbiosis And Individuation* (New York: Basic Books, 1975).

5. KEEP YOUR ANXIETY FROM RUNNING THE SHOW

1 Rick Hanson, *Hardwiring Happiness: The New Brain Science of Contentment, Calm, and Confidence* (New York: Harmony, 2013).

2 Harriet Lerner, *The Dance of Anger: A Woman's Guide to Changing the Patterns of Intimate Relationships* (New York: Harper & Row, 1989), 222.

3 James Maddock, in consultation, 2001. Jim was heavily influenced by the work of Murray Bowen who said, "When a person is emotionally involved in a situation or subject . . . the thinking response can be overwhelmed by intense feeling and emotional responses. These feeling and emotional reactions occur so quickly that they appear to envelop and modify the thinking response. . . . Sometimes people are aware that their thinking is altered by feelings and emotions, but more often the subtleness of the process precludes awareness." In Michael E. Kerr and Murray Bowen, *Family Evaluation* (New York: W.W. Norton, 1988), 60.

4   Kerr and Bowen, *Family Evaluation*.

5   My paraphrasing of Kerr and Bowen's definition. Kerr and Bowen, *Family Evaluation*, 112.

6   Harriet Lerner, *The Dance of Anger*.

7   David Schnarch refers to this as "begrudging respect: Not begrudging in the sense of discontented or resentful . . . begrudging as in hard-earned admiration. . . . Mutual respect based on strength." David Schnarch, *Passionate Marriage: Love, Sex, and Intimacy in Emotionally Committed Relationships* (New York: W.W. Norton, 1997), 205.

6. WHAT HAPPENS ONCE YOU CALM DOWN?

1   The material in this section owes much to the Family Systems Theory of Murray Bowen as well as the work of Ellyn Bader, Peter Pearson, Harriet Lerner, and David Schnarch. This section's heading is drawn from Harriet Lerner's *The Dance of Connection*.

2   Michael E. Kerr and Murray Bowen, *Family Evaluation* (New York: W.W. Norton, 1988).

3   James Maddock, in consultation, 2002, based on the work of Murray Bowen; Kerr and Bowen, *Family Evaluation*.

4   Harriet Lerner, *The Dance of Connection: How to Talk to Someone When You're Mad, Hurt, Scared, Frustrated, Insulted, Betrayed, or Desperate* (New York: HarperCollins, 2002), 105.

5   Kerr and Bowen, *Family Evaluation*, 116.

6   Kerr and Bowen, *Family Evaluation*; Pema Chödrön, *The Places that Scare You: A Guide to Fearlessness in Difficult Times* (Boston: Shambala Publications, 2001).

7   References to *self-soothing* and *self-regulation* appear throughout the psychological literature, with different theoretical orientations offering their unique explanations of how we develop the capacity to self-soothe in the presence of anxiety.

   Some suggest that we derive this ability by internalizing the validation and support of others. This implies that self-soothing involves or depends on an external source of comfort. Differentiation-based theorists believe that we learn to self-soothe out of necessity. As we struggle to define ourselves despite pressure from others to behave and think as they prefer and grow increasingly able to tolerate anxiety and separateness, we come to rely on our inner resources to soothe ourselves when we are anxious.

Bowen preferred the term *self-regulation*, noting that although the process of differentiation ultimately leads us to a more solid sense of self and a greater ability to self-soothe, the work it entails is often anxiety-provoking. Managing our emotional reactivity and learning to comfort ourselves in the face of disappointment are hardly experiences that one would consider to be *soothing*.

See Kerr and Bowen, *Family Evaluation*; Joanne Wright, "Self-Soothing—A Recursive Intrapsychic and Relational Process: The Contribution of the Bowen Theory to the Process of Self-Soothing," *Australian and New Zealand Journal of Family Therapy* 30 no. 1 (2009): 29–41; David Schnarch, *Passionate Marriage: Sex, Love, and Intimacy in Emotionally Committed Relationships* (New York: Norton, 1997).

8   Virginia Todd Holeman, *Reconcilable Differences: Hope and Healing for Troubled Marriages* (Downers Grove, IL: InterVarsity Press, 2004), 115–16.

9   Robert Firestone, Lisa Firestone, and Joyce Catlett, *The Self Under Siege: A Therapeutic Model for Differentiation* (New York: Routledge, 2013); David Schnarch, *Constructing the Sexual Crucible: An Integration of Sexual and Marital Therapy* (New York: W.W. Norton, 1991); Ellyn Bader and Peter Pearson, The Couples Institute training materials (Menlo Park, CA, 1992).

10   David Schnarch, *Passionate Marriage*; Sue Johnson, *Love Sense: The Revolutionary New Science of Romantic Relationships* (New York: Hachette, 2013).

11   Murray Bowen, *Family Therapy in Clinical Practice* (Lanham, MD: Rowman & Littlefield, 1978); David Schnarch, *Passionate Marriage*.

NOTES

9. MARRIAGE IS A CHOICE

1 To learn more about maintaining intimacy and passion, see David Schnarch, *Passionate Marriage: Sex, Love, and Intimacy in Emotionally Committed Relationships* (New York: Norton, 1997).

11. 360 DEGREES AND SUNNY

1 Murray Bowen, *Family Therapy in Clinical Practice* (Lanham, MD: Rowman & Littlefield, 1978), 95. Here, Bowen talks about "the responsible 'I' which assumes responsibility for [one's own actions, thoughts and feelings, and] one's own happiness and comfort and well-being. [The responsible 'I'] avoids thinking that tends to blame one's own unhappiness, discomfort, or failure on the other."

2 Rick Hanson, *Hardwiring Happiness: The New Brain Science of Contentment, Calm, and Confidence* (New York: Harmony, 2013).

ABOUT THE AUTHOR

Winifred M. Reilly is a marriage and family therapist, with a private practice in Berkeley, California. In her thirty-five years of clinical practice she has treated hundreds of couples—many of whom felt certain they were headed for divorce. Winifred has been a guest lecturer on marriage and sexuality, and her writing has appeared on *The Huffington Post*, *The Good Men Project*, *xoJane*, and on her relationship advice blog, *Speaking of Marriage*.